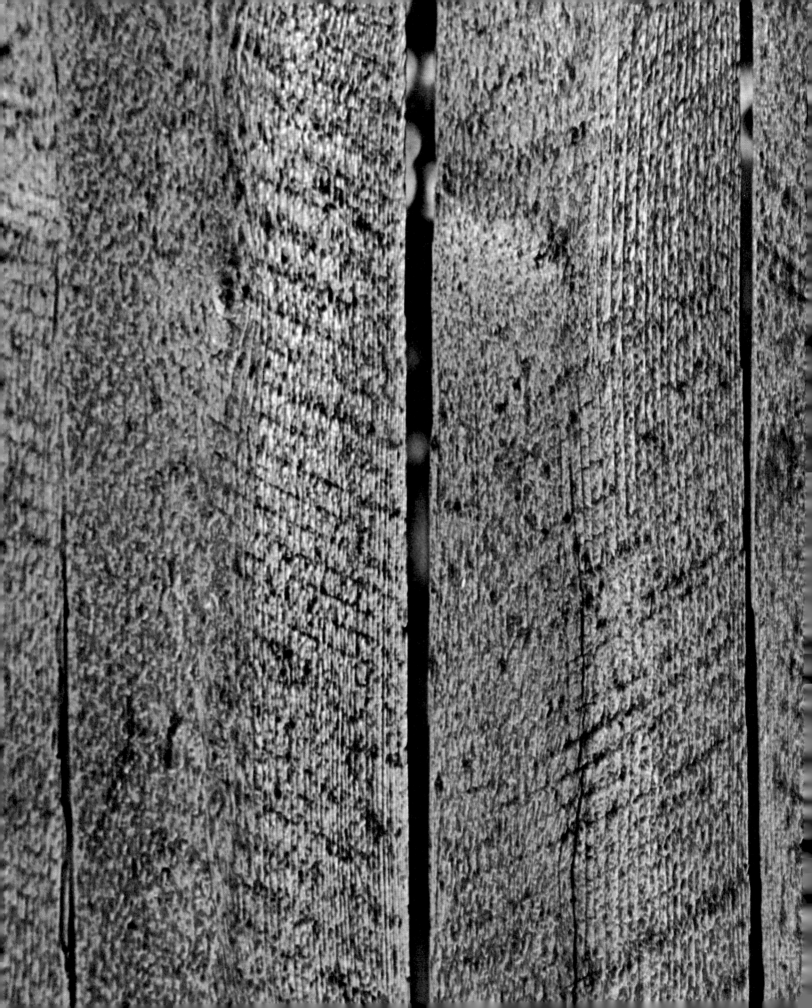

THE FAMILY CREATIVE WORKSHOP

20

Tea, Terrariums
Terrines and Timbales, Tie Dyeing
Time Telling, Tin and Pierced Work
Tin Painting, Topiary
Totem Poles, Toys

Plenary Publications International, Inc.
New York and Amsterdam

Published by Plenary Publications International, Incorporated 10 East 49th Street, New York, New York 10017, for the Blue Mountain Crafts Council.

Library of Congress Catalog Card Number: 73-89331. Complete set International Standard Book Number: 0-88459-021-6. Volume 20 International Standard Book Number: 0-88459-019-4.

Manufactured in the United States of America. Printed and bound by the W.A. Krueger Company, Brookfield, Wisconsin.

Printing preparation by Lanman Lithoplate Company.

Publishers:
Plenary Publications International, Incorporated 10 East 49th Street New York, New York 10017

James Wagenvoord
EDITOR-IN-CHIEF

Jerry Curcio
PRODUCTION MANAGER

Jo Springer
VOLUME EDITOR

Joanne Delaney
Ellen Foley
EDITORIAL ASSISTANTS

Editorial preparation:
Tree Communications, Inc. 250 Park Avenue South New York, New York 10003

Rodney Friedman
EDITORIAL DIRECTOR

Ronald Gross
DESIGN DIRECTOR

Paul Levin
DIRECTOR OF PHOTOGRAPHY

Jill Munves
TEXT EDITOR

Sonja Douglas
ART DIRECTOR

Rochelle Lapidus
Marsha Gold
DESIGNERS

Lucille O'Brien
EDITORIAL PRODUCTION

Ruth Forst Michel
COPYREADER

Eva Gold
ADMINISTRATIVE MANAGER

Editors for this volume:
Andrea DiNoto
TERRARIUMS
TERRINES AND TIMBALES

Donal Dinwiddie
TOYS

Michael Donner
TIME TELLING
TOPIARY
TOTEM POLES

Linda Hetzer
TEA

Nancy Bruning Levine
TIN PAINTING

Marilyn Nierenberg
TIE DYEING
TIN AND PIERCED WORK

Originating editor of the series:
Allen Davenport Bragdon

Contributing editors:
Barbara Daye
Dennis Starin
Gen Ventrone

Contributing illustrators:
Marina Givotovsky
Patricia Lee
Lynn Matus
Sally Shimizu

Contributing photographers:
Bob Jones
Steven Mays
Bruce Schlein
Dennis Starin

Production:
Thom Augusta
Christopher Jones
Patricia Lee
Sylvia Sherwin
Leslie Strong
Gregory Wong

Photo and illustration credits:
TEA: Etchings, pages 2440 and 2446, courtesy of the New York Public Library Picture Collection; Japanese calligraphy, pages 2448, 2450, and 2451, by Ippei Shimizu. TIE DYEING: Illustrations, pages 2474, 2475, and 2479, by Eileen Richardson; Indian tie dye, page 2472 and rice tie dye, page 2488, courtesy of India Nepal Handloom House, New York, New York; scarf, page 2471, and caftan, page 2489, designed by the Richardsons, courtesy of Rit Dye, Best Foods Division, CPC International, Indianapolis, Indiana; tissue-paper tie dye, page 2488, designed by Marilyn Nierenberg; African tie dye, page 2473, courtesy of Sonja Douglas. TOTEM POLES: Photographs, pages 2544 and 2545 (right), courtesy of Alaska Division of Tourism.

Acknowledgements:
TIE DYEING: The editors wish to thank Allison Stooker of the Softness Group (Rit Dye), New York, New York for her assistance. TOTEM POLES: Technical consultant, Glenn Holder.

The Project-Evaluation Symbols appearing in the title heading at the beginning of each project have these meanings:

Range of approximate cost:
¢ Low: under $5 or free and found natural materials

$ Medium: about $10

$$ High: above $15

Estimated time to completion for an unskilled adult:
Hours

Days

Weeks

Suggested level of experience:
Child alone

Supervised child or family project

Unskilled adult

Specialized prior training

Tools and equipment:
Small hand tools

Large hand and household tools

Specialized or powered equipment

On the cover:
This tie-dye design is a detail of the chiffon caftan shown on page 2489. With a combination of some of the basic knots and folds illustrated in the Craftnotes on pages 2474 and 2475, almost any fabric that will absorb dye can be decorated with swirls of dazzling color. Cover photograph by Steven Mays.

**Contents and
Craftspeople for
Volume 20:**

TEA
The Healthful Brew

A cup of tea, whether it be your favorite herbal concoction, a pleasing blend of black tea, or a packaged brand from the supermarket, is always an enjoyable refreshment. But it becomes more rewarding in proportion to the amount of time spent in the selection and preparation of the brew. It becomes even more enjoyable if you have grown, then picked, dried, and prepared your own ingredients; and then share the herbal brew with friends.

A Medicinal Beginning

Tea drinking—including both herbal and black teas—began because it was thought to cure various ailments. It was from this medicinal beginning that black tea grew to become the most important beverage in the Far East. One of the earliest references to tea was in a medical book that supposedly dates to 2737 B.C. Tea was described by the Chinese Emperor Shen Nung as having properties which ranged from the ability to cure ailments to its uplifting effect on body and spirit. This book, *Pen-ts'ao*, also lists more than three hundred herbal preparations, making it the oldest compilation of herbal remedies in existence.

Herbal teas are mentioned in the ancient histories of many cultures. According to the Ebers Papyrus, an ancient Egyptian record, there were 2,000 herb doctors in Egypt 20 centuries before Christ. And there are references to herbal cures in the Old Testament. Throughout the ages, many herbals were published containing specific concoctions to use in treating certain maladies.

Herb Teas

To many people, the word herbs conjures up a warm cup of tea rather than a food seasoning. A number of herbs have such consistently pleasant flavors that they can be enjoyed often by themselves or combined with each other. More than 20 old favorites are listed and described on pages 2444 and 2445.

Victor Werbin is a native New Yorker. He moved to Colorado in 1970, where he lives on a 7,200-foot mountain west of Boulder in a cabin with no phone, electricity, gas, or running water. He heats the cabin with fireplace wood he chops, and works as an herb mixer for Celestial Seasonings, a tea manufacturer.

Greenery and Growing Things
Herb cultivation

Herbs, unlike many vegetables, fruits, and flowers, have not been highly cultivated by modern man. They still grow in their original wild state. So they grow best in a climate and soil similar to those in which they originated.

Most herbs seem to have come from around the Mediterranean Sea. Sunny, temperate climates induce good growth if the soil is well drained and there is even rainfall through the growing season. Such conditions are the norm throughout most of the United States and Europe, though most herbs do not prosper along the Gulf Coast or in Florida. A particularly rich soil is not essential, although many herbs do thrive in rich, black soil. Herbs are very adaptable plants.

The well-drained soil that herbs need will hold moisture but not trap it. When drainage is poor, water will either run off the top of the soil or soak quickly through it, beyond the reach of plant roots. Lack of sufficient organic matter is the most common cause of poor drainage. It is usually the organic matter that holds water and keeps the soil from caking on top or powdering. You can correct poor drainage by adding manure, compost, peat, or other organic materials. Manure and compost also have food value for plants, of course, but herbs do not need much feeding if the climate and drainage are suitable. In fact, many seem to thrive in soils where little else will grow.

The pleasure of a warming cup of tea has traveled around the world from the place of its discovery in the Far East. It has become a popular drink in almost every country in the world, but is especially popular in China, Japan, India, Russia, and Great Britain.

In colonial America, herb teas were called tisanes; they were adopted for both economic and political reasons. Imported tea from England was expensive, and taxes made it more so. Many women in the colonies concocted an infusion of raspberry leaves as a beverage to protest these taxes. Tea made from wild plants that grew in America became known as "liberty tea."

A teapot stand patented by Thomas D. Currier of Waldoboro, Maine, on November 14, 1871, allows the pot to be carried and used without burning the hands.

Herb Classification

Which herbs should you plant? There are three basic classifications: annuals (including basil, coriander, marjoram, camomile); biennials (including sage, mullein); and perennials (including rosemary, catnip, fennel). The annuals must be planted every year; they grow, produce seed, and die in a single season. In many cases, of course, they self-seed and come up year after year. When you grow annuals, you can change your selection every year. Biennials produce leaves which can be used the first season, but they do not flower and die until the second season after planting. If you plant biennials every year, you will assure a flowering crop each fall. Perennials last for many years if they are given reasonable care.

There are three basic means of propagating herbs—from seeds, from cuttings, and from root divisions. If you start herbs from seed, remember that growth will take a good deal of time—sometimes longer than a growing season. So start the herb seedlings indoors as early as March. But do not start earlier than that; a plant kept indoors too long will not have the strength it needs to survive transplanting outdoors. Sage, camomile, anise, and catnip can best be propagated from seeds. You can start herb seeds indoors in containers of sterile potting soil, or germinate them first in sphagnum moss and sand or some other porous but nonnutritive soil mixture. Place the seeds in rows ¼ inch deep, but leave them uncovered. Mist them three times a day, shade them with a few sheets of newspaper, and keep them in a room with a temperature near 70 degrees Fahrenheit. Once the seeds form their first leaves, move them into regular potting soil in single pots or spaced no less than 1¼ inches apart in seed flats. The plants should be ready for transplanting into larger pots after three to four weeks and ready for the garden a few weeks later, depending on the weather.

Propagation from Cuttings

Many herbs are propagated from stem cuttings, including peppermint, spearmint, and rosemary. This is an easy and convenient way to multiply plants. A cutting is a sprig about 3 inches long, taken from the tip of a branch during the growing season. Remove the bottom leaves, leaving the upper 1½ inches intact. Put the cutting in a very absorbent medium (sphagnum moss is good) which also contains some humus or compost. Dip the cutting in hormone rooting powder before you insert it in the pot. Give the cuttings plenty of room, and mist them a few times daily. It is also important that the soil be kept warm—at least 65 degrees Fahrenheit. Within a few weeks, roots and new leaves will develop.

Division is a very simple way to propagate perennials. What you are doing is splitting a mature plant into pieces and replanting them. Of course one must have mature plants available to use this method. Herbs best propagated by division include hyssop and lemon balm. Dig up the plant, preferably in early spring before new growth starts, and shake the dirt from the roots. It is best to do this when it is neither sunny nor windy. Divide the plant with a spade so you retain a good root system for each new plant. Replant these sections in the soil as you would any transplant.

Once the herbs are growing in the garden give them the same care afforded vegetables—watering, cultivating, and weeding. Most important, though, is to provide a good surface mulch. This can be hay, grass clippings, leaves, bark, or other light organic material. This will hold the water in and keep the weeds down.

Harvesting Herbs

Leaf drying is the most common method of preserving herbs. The herbs should be harvested just before or when they begin to flower. It is then that they have the most abundant oil. Flowers do not all develop at once, of course; so the harvest can continue over a period of time. Perennials need to be harvested early enough so they can establish new growth before frost; leave at least two sets of leaves at the base of the stalks when you cut. Annuals can be pulled roots and all unless you want some plants to reseed themselves. In that case a few plants should be left untouched.

Harvest herbs in the morning, just after the dew has left the plants. At that time the oils are strongest. Once you cut the herbs, prepare them for drying as quickly as possible. Wash the plants, if necessary, and separate leaves and tops from the heavier stems to speed drying.

Drying is a simple process. Always dry herbs in a well-ventilated place away from direct sunlight. A familiar drying method (Figure A) is to fasten a bunch of plants together at the bottom of the stems and hang them upside down. (If you use elastic bands, the herbs will not drop out of the bunch as the stems shrink.) This is a good method if you can keep the bunches loose to permit air to flow through. Take care not to knock off the dry, fragile leaves as you handle the herbs during and after drying.

For herb leaves which have been stripped from their stems, there are two good methods of drying. Herbs may be placed in paper bags (not plastic) for drying (Figure B). This is a good method for flower tops (such as red clover) and seed clusters (such as dill or fennel). Leave the bag open at the top and suspend it so the

Dried herbal tea should always be kept in an airtight container. A container of clear glass with a cork top lets you admire the beauty of the colorful herbs.

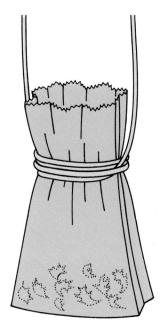

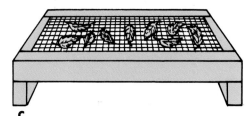

A
Figure A: The simplest method of drying herbs is to fasten them together into loose bunches with a cord or elastic band and hang them upside down in a cool, airy place.

B
Figure B: A good way to dry flower tops and seed heads is to place them in a paper bag. Leave the bag open at the top and suspend it so air can circulate around the flowers.

C
Figure C: The drying screen is a drying method for loose leaves, stripped from a stem. Spread the thin layer of herbs on a fine-mesh screen where air can circulate above and below.

bottom does not touch the ground. Do not fill the bag very full. In screen drying (Figure C), simply spread the foliage thinly on a fine-mesh screen, with space above and below for air circulation. Never put the screen directly on the ground or a shelf. Spread paper below the screen to catch any herbs that dry up, crumble, and fall through the mesh.

After the herbs are completely dry, place them in sealed jars or plastic bags. Check the containers a few times after sealing them. If there is moisture on the sides, the herbs were not dry enough; remove them for further drying. Store the containers away from direct sunlight.

Blending Herbs for Tea

If you want to blend an herb tea, you need to know which herbs have similar qualities. One way to categorize the herb teas is to divide them by taste—earthy, sweet, citrus and coffeelike. Earthy herbs include alfalfa, red clover blossoms, comfrey, dandelion leaves, hawthorn berries, mullein, papaya leaves, and yarrow flowers. Sweet herbs—also somewhat earthy—are all the mints, camomile, linden flowers, and all the berry leaves. Citrus flavors are obtained from lemon grass, lemon peel, orange peel, orange leaves, and orange blossoms. Coffeelike herbs include dandelion root, chicory root, roasted barley, roasted barley malt, and crystal malt. The simplest blends are mixtures of similar flavors.

When you cross the lines of similarity, the real adventure of blending begins for

Herb tea recipes

A refreshing afternoon tea

1 part spearmint
1 part red clover blossoms
1 part camomile

A mellow evening tea

5 parts camomile
1 part skullcap
1 part passion flowers
1 part hawthorn berries
1 part life-everlasting
1 part spearmint

A tea blend that includes all categories

2 parts rose hips
2 parts camomile
2 parts red clover blossoms
1 part lemon grass
½ part orange peel

These colorful dried herbs are, from top to bottom, licorice root, hibiscus flowers, camomile, rose hips, comfrey leaves, star anise, and peppermint.

you. Start with a base of herbs from one category, then add other flavors to it. The base is usually one-third of the total used, but it can be as much as one-half if you want one flavor to dominate. For an earthy blend, for example, start with a base of red clover and alfalfa for one-third of the mixture; then add spearmint, camomile and comfrey. Other earthy bases are camomile and comfrey, or comfrey and berry leaves. For a sweet taste, try adding anise seed or licorice to an earthy base.

One citrus base is a mixture of rose hips and hibiscus. Any of the berry leaves make a smooth background for such citrus flavors; a good combination is made of equal parts of lemon grass and strawberry leaves. Any of the mints can also be added to a citrus-flavored base. Another good base—this one sweet—is a combination of any of the mints with any of the berry leaves. The berry leaves seem to make good backgrounds for almost any flavor. They contain the qualities of more than one group, and at one time can be fruity, sweet, earthy, and aromatic.

The rich, brown, coffeelike herbs are usually blended only with one another. Try equal parts of chicory root, dandelion root, roasted barley, and crystal malt. There is one earthy herb, maté, that does blend well with these herbs.

Once you become familiar with the way the flavor groups complement each other, you are well on the way to finding herbs that will round out the blend you are seeking. You may find, for example, that when you blend camomile and spearmint, you have a flavorful blend but one that is hard to keep in balance, with one of the two herbs tending to overshadow the other. If a mellow background herb, such as one of the berry leaves or comfrey, is added, you can make a smoother tea.

Some people, for example, find rose hips and camomile a good blend, but the divergence of these flavors is too much for others. I came across my favorite blends by intuition and experimentation, and I find it is very satisfying to create personal blends this way.

Kitchen Favorites and Celebrations
Brewing tea

As important as the selection and blending of herbal tea is the brewing process itself. Leaves, flowers, and seeds of herbs, and all Indian teas should not be boiled, only steeped. Boiling destroys the nutritional value and much of the flavor. But the water should be boiling hot when the tea is added, so maximum flavor is extracted and it should always be fresh; reheated water imparts a flat taste. (Roots and barks may be boiled or steeped; try both ways.) When you steep herbs, use a separate vessel for boiling the water and a teapot for the steeping. Or the tea can be steeped one cup at a time if you use a tea strainer deep enough to allow hot water to surround the herbs.

Utensils
The use of an aluminum kettle to boil the water is not advisable; the aluminum tends to leach into the water and contaminate the tea. Scratched or scoured steel can have the same effect. Use a well-kept stainless-steel kettle, an enameled kettle of good quality, or a copper kettle.

The teapot you use can be made of china or ceramic; both treat herbs kindly. But if you buy a ceramic pot, make certain it has a lead-free glaze. Most metal teapots affect the flavor of herb tea and radiate heat out instead of holding it in. Avoid putting your tea inside a tea ball for steeping; that restricts the flow of the water and decreases the quality of the brew.

There are two types of tea strainers available, stainless steel and bamboo. The bamboo strainer is more pleasing to look at, but sometimes a finer mesh can be obtained with stainless steel. Either works well when you strain tea poured from a teapot. The bamboo strainer is better when you steep one cup of tea because it allows more hot water to flow through the tea.

Making the Tea
Before brewing the tea, warm and freshen the teapot by rinsing it with hot water. Then none of the heat of the tea water will be lost in heating a cold pot. Place the herbs in the teapot. Measure carefully, using 1 to 1½ teaspoons for each cup of tea

(photograph 1) (or one for each cup and one for the pot). Pour freshly boiled water over them (photograph 2). It takes time for the qualities of herbs to be carried into the hot water, but too long a steeping time creates a bitter tea. About seven minutes is a good length of time for most herbs; black teas can steep a shorter time, three to five minutes. Herbs that must be boiled usually are processed for a longer time—about 20 minutes.

1: To make tea, warm the teapot by rinsing it with hot water; then measure the herbs carefully into the pot.

2: Pour freshly boiled water over the herbs, and let them steep for about seven minutes to bring out the flavor and nutrients.

3: Strain the tea into your cup, using a strainer reserved for tea. A strainer used for other things will affect the taste of the tea.

Once the tea has been steeped or boiled, strain it into your cup (photograph 3). Always use a strainer that is used only for tea. One used for other purposes will change the flavor of the tea. Even if your teapot has a built-in strainer, use a separate strainer, too. Then season your tea if you like. Traditionally, milk is not used with herb teas, but you might like a little honey and lemon juice. If the tea is too strong, dilute it with hot water after it is strained. And judge its strength by taste, not color.

Herbal teas, as well as Indian tea, can be used to make a refreshing summer drink. To make herbal iced tea, begin as you do for hot tea, but increase the amount of tea per cup by 50 percent. This allows for dilution by the melting ice. Let the tea steep for seven minutes, strain it, and let it stand until it has cooled to room temperature. If you put the hot tea directly into the refrigerator, it may get cloudy. To serve, pour the cooled tea over ice cubes.

Traditionally, herb teas are sweetened with a little honey or flavored with honey and lemon juice, but are never diluted with milk.

For further reading

American Medicinal Plants by Charles F. Millspaugh, Dover Publications, Inc., New York.

The Book of Tea by Kakuzo Okakura, Dover Publications, Inc., New York.

Common and Uncommon Uses of Herbs by Richard Lucas, Arco Publishing Co., Inc., New York.

The Golden Age of Herbs and Herbalists by Rosetta E. Clarkson, Dover Publications, Inc., New York.

The Herb Book by John Lust, Bantam Books, Inc., New York.

A Modern Herbal, Volumes 1 and 2, by Mrs. M. Grieve, Dover Publications, Inc., New York.

Pharmacognosy by Edward P. Claus, Lea & Febiger, Philadelphia, Pa.

The Rodale Herb Book by William H. Hylton, Rodale Press, Emmaus, Pa.

Angelica (Angelica archangelica), perennial: grows in very moist, shady areas, especially near running water. Use leaves or roots to make tea.

Camomile (Anthemis nobilis), perennial: needs lots of sun. Use the tiny flowers to make a sweet-smelling and soothing tea.

Lemon balm (Melissa officinalis), perennial: grows in full sun or partial shade, tends to spread. Strong lemon-scented leaves make a citrus tea.

Anise (Pimpinella anisum), annual: grows in warm, dry, sunny areas. Used by the Egyptians and the Romans as a flavoring for cake. Use slightly bruised seeds for tea.

Comfrey (Symphytum officinale), perennial: needs a moist, shady area. Use the leaves to make an earthy tea. Historically used to clear up mucous conditions and as a dressing for wounds.

Licorice (Glycyrrhiza glabra), perennial: grows best in sandy soil near streams. Extract from the roots was used as a cold remedy in the Middle Ages. The roots also make a very sweet, thick tea.

Bergamot (Monarda didyma), perennial: flowers best in moist soil with morning sun only. Tea made from fresh or dried leaves is known as Oswego tea because the plant grew wild near Oswego, New York, when settlers arrived in America.

Lime flowers (Tilia Europoea), tree: also known as linden flowers. The flowers of this tree (not the common fruit) make a sweet, perfumed tea.

Hibiscus (Althea rosea), tender shrub: indigenous to China. The flowers can be used to make a red dye as well as a fragrant tea.

Catnip (Nepeta cataria), perennial: also known as catmint. Grows easily and does not need any special attention. Has an aroma that cats are fond of. Use the flowers to make tea.

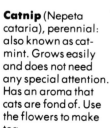

Hyssop flowers (Hyssopus officinalis), perennial: an evergreen that grows best in warm, dry soil. Use the flowers to make tea.

Maté (Ilex paraguayensis), shrub: also known as Yerba maté or Paraguay herb. Grows wild near streams in South America. Tea made from the leaves is bitter tasting, contains caffeine and minerals, and is a popular drink in many parts of South America.

HERBS FOR TEA

Nettle (Urtica dioica), perennial: the plant is known as the stinging nettle due to its sharp pointed leaves. Tea made from the leaves contains some Vitamin A.

Rosemary (Rosmarinus officinalis), perennial: needs full sun and moist, well-drained soil. Use fresh leaves to make tea with a pinelike aroma.

Strawberry

Peppermint (Mentha piperita), perennial: grows in warm, moist soil rich in humus. Most familiar of the mints; leaves make a tea that has a sweet aroma and a menthol taste.

Sage (Salvia officinalis), perennial: grows in warm, dry soil in the shade. Name derived from Latin **salvere**, to be saved, referring to the curative properties associated with it. Tea made from the dried leaves was preferred by some Chinese to tea from the tea plant.

Raspberry

Red clover (Trifolium pratense), perennial: grows best in sandy soil. Tea made from the blossoms contains some iron.

Spearmint (Mentha viridis), perennial: a hardy plant that grows best in moist, cool areas. Tea made from dried leaves has greater nuances of flavor than does the more common peppermint tea.

Blueberry

Rose hips (Rosaceae), shrub: for centuries, the rose was not only admired for its beauty and fragrance, but also for its medicinal purposes. The hips, or seed cases, which form after the flowers have bloomed are rich in vitamin C. Tea made from dried rose hips is citrus flavored and red in color.

Thyme (Thymus serpyllum), perennial: prefers light, sandy soil. Tea made from dried leaves is believed to be good for the digestion.

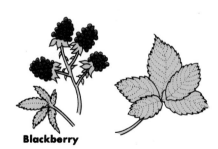

Blackberry

Berry leaves. The leaves of strawberry, raspberry, blueberry, and blackberry plants all make fruity teas. They can be added to other herbs for an added fruity taste.

The original tea plant

The traditional tea of the Far East comes from an evergreen herb, thea sinensis, related to the Camellia family. It grows wild in one area, where Tibet, India, China, and Burma meet. Though it will grow almost anywhere, it will produce a good tea leaf only under certain conditions—a warm climate with plenty of rain. All of the various types of black, brown, and green teas come from the same plant. There are slight differences in flavor, which probably stem from variations in climate and soil where the tea was grown. In India, the plant could grow into a tree 30 feet tall, but it is not allowed to do so for that would decrease the quality of the tea. Instead it is kept about four feet tall so the plant's energy will be directed toward the growth of abundant leaves.

The drying process

The major differences one finds in teas are a result of the processing they go through after harvest. The first stage for all black teas is wilting—the initial drying stage. The leaves are spread thinly and are evenly heated, either naturally or by the use of hot air. After wilting the black tea leaves are crushed by rollers. The leaf is twisted and damaged to release the juices that start the fermentation process. (Green tea does not go through the wilting process. It is put immediately into firing machines to keep it from fermenting. Then the green tea is also rolled, but fermentation has already been arrested.) For fermentation the rolled leaves of black tea are spread on a cement or tiled surface in a cool, damp atmosphere. Through oxidation, the leaves turn a bright copper color and gain the flavor which distinguishes them from green tea.

The leaves are now ready for the firing process that halts the fermentation. The tea is placed on trays in a large iron box. These trays move slowly from top to bottom, with great care being taken to make sure the leaves are dried evenly and not scorched. The tea emerges in its final black state.

Oolong tea is a special kind that is a compromise between the black and green teas. The leaf is withered slightly like black tea, but like green tea, it is heat-dried before it is rolled. This produces a greenish-brown tea.

The drying process is now complete, but the tea still has a few steps it must go through before packaging. These are the sorting processes. The leaves are separated into various grades, ranging from the leaf grades to broken grades. For instance, orange pekoe (pronounced peck-o, not peek-o) simply refers to the youngest leaves opened at the top of the plant. The only tea that is finer is flowery pekoe, made from leaf buds that have not yet opened. Because these small leaves are intact, not as much surface area is exposed to boiling water when the tea is steeped in comparison with broken cuts. So the leaves produce a lighter, paler tea.

Grades by leaf size

The other two grades of leaf tea are pekoe and souchong. The pekoe leaves grow near the top and are a bit larger than those of orange pekoe. The souchong, next on the stem, is a much rounder and larger leaf, but like orange pekoe and pekoe, produces a pale, delicate tea.

Next comes broken orange pekoe. It is in much smaller fragments than the leaf grades, producing a stronger cup of tea. Broken pekoe is larger than broken orange pekoe and produces a slightly lighter cup of tea. The broken souchong is larger still and produces an even lighter cup of tea. After these grades come smaller pieces and dust, both very quick-brewing cuts of tea. They are often used in tea bags.

The other names that one finds on tea packages refer to the place where the tea grew. The same tea plants grown in different locations produce varying flavors of tea. So when you consider the major types (black, green, or oolong), the many cuts, and the many locations where tea is grown, the selection is broad.

A drawing of professional tea-tasters deciding on the quality of a new shipment of tea was published in 1879 in a series called "Life Sketches in the Metropolis."

Performing Arts
The Japanese tea ceremony

Duane Feasel became interested in Japanese architecture and gardens while he was in high school in Los Angeles. After seeing a display of tea utensils, he studied the tea ceremony once a week for seven years. During this time, he was graduated from the University of Southern California and became a music teacher. He received a scholarship to the Urasenke School in Kyoto, Japan, and studied there for three years. He lived in a dormitory with Japanese students so he learned to speak fluent Japanese. After graduation, he was sent to New York to teach, the only American ever hired by the Urasenke School to teach the tea ceremony.

Tea drinking came to Japan through China. The scholar, Gan Lu, of the later Han period (25-221 A.D.) is credited with the introduction of tea to China. He traveled to India to study Indian culture and brought back both Buddhism and tea, thus establishing an early link between tea drinking and religious ceremony. To this day in China, and even more so in Japan, tea drinking is surrounded with symbolism.

By the fourth century A.D., references to tea are common in Chinese literature, and in the fifth century a Chinese dictionary, the *Kuang-fa*, describes tea as a pleasant drink, rather than just a medicine. By the seventh century A.D. tea became an export item for the Chinese.

The tea trade led to the first major treatise on tea when merchants of the eighth century induced Lu Yu to write on the subject. His work, called the *Ch'a Ching* (Tea Classic), appeared around 780 A.D. It dealt with tea drinking, brewing and serving utensils, preparation, history, and once again emphasized the teachings of Buddhism and the Tao in connection with tea drinking.

It was during the Sung period (960-1127 A.D.) that tea was elevated to its present status in the Far East. During this period, China turned away from foreign influences and concentrated on what it considered to be its own culture. Tea drinking was stressed for this reason. It was also during this period that Zen Buddhists incorporated tea drinking into their ceremonies and meditations. These ceremonial aspects later led to the famous Japanese tea ceremony.

Tea arrived in Japan around the seventh century, brought by Japanese Buddhist monks who had been sent to China to study with Chinese masters.

The Tea Ceremony

The Japanese tea ceremony, called *Chanoyu* has elevated the making of a bowl of tea and the sharing of it to the level of an art form. The tea ceremony was developed by Zen Buddhist monks. The earliest tea drinkers of China were such monks, who drank tea to help them stay awake during long meditations. So the tea became associated with the spiritual aspects of their lives.

When tea reached Japan, it came with Buddhism. The tea ceremony was initiated during the periods of Higashiyama and Monoyama (late fifteenth and early sixteenth centuries). But it was a tea master, Sen No Rikyu (1522-1590), who shaped the way of tea, a religion of daily life. The four elements of his tea ceremony were harmony, respect, purity, and tranquility.

The ceremony as practiced then and now has a specific procedure. The tea room, which originated as a room set aside for this purpose inside a house, later became a separate teahouse with three rooms: a room for the sharing of the tea, an anteroom in which utensils are kept, and a portico or waiting room for guests.

There are rarely more than five guests. When they have assembled, they sound a wooden gong to alert the host. When they enter the tea-sharing room, there is no talk of worldly matters but rather a discussion of aspects of the ceremony. The guests are carefully selected to ensure compatability and tranquillity. The guests admire a scroll (one selected that is appropriate for them and for the season) and a flower arrangement. A tea kettle and heat source are in the room. The host brings in the tea utensils—an earthenware water jar, a lacquerware tea caddy, a bowl, a linen cloth, a bamboo teaspoon, a bamboo dipper, a whisk, a receptacle for the water, and a silk napkin. He also brings in a plate of sweet cookies.

The scroll and flower are the only decorations used in the tea ceremony. The Japanese words on this scroll read, from top to bottom, pure, autumn, geese, south, fly. The guests contemplate these objects.

Making the Tea

To begin making tea, the host picks up the dipper with a precise, balletlike movement (photograph 4, page 2450). He purifies the tea caddy by wiping it with a folded cloth (photograph 5). He purifies the bamboo teaspoon with this folded cloth (photograph 6). The tea bowl is warmed with water from the kettle; then the whisk is rinsed in the bowl. The water is put into the receptacle, and the bowl is dried with the linen cloth. The utensils are now ready for making tea. The host gestures to the guests to eat a sweet cookie because a sweet taste in the mouth is supposed to heighten the taste of the tea.

To make the tea, the host measures the powdered green tea into the tea bowl, using the bamboo teaspoon (photograph 7). He uses the dipper to transfer hot water from the kettle to the bowl (photograph 8). Then he stirs the tea vigorously with the whisk until it is foamy (photograph 9). When the tea is ready, the host offers the bowl to the first guest. The host and the guest bow to each other (photograph 10). The guest picks up the bowl of tea, turns it so she does not drink from the front of the bowl, then drinks (photograph 11). It is good etiquette to drink all the tea. The guest may then admire the bowl and ask the host about its origin (photograph 12). The host makes a bowl of tea for each guest in turn.

Respect for the beauty of the utensils is carried to the end of the ceremony, when the host cleans each of the utensils as the guests watch. It is much the same process as was purifying them in the beginning. The host carries the utensils out of the tea room as clean as they were when brought in.

For related entries, see "Herbs" and "Organic Gardening."

This is the Japanese symbol for tea.

The utensils used for the tea ceremony are special and are reserved for this occasion. They are put in particular positions; this is the position before the host makes the tea.

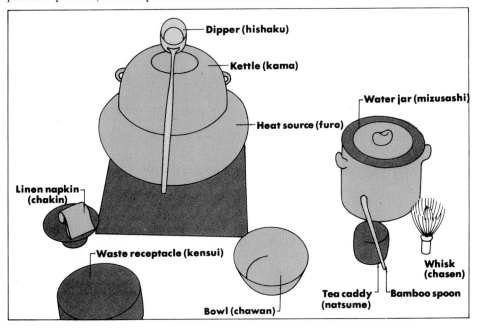

The utensils for the tea ceremony shown in the photograph at the top of the page are identified with their Japanese names in the drawing above.

4: The host picks up the dipper in a precise movement. The tea ceremony begins.

5: He purifies the lacquerware tea caddy by wiping it gently with a folded cloth.

6: The same cloth, folded similarly, is used to purify the bamboo teaspoon.

7: To make the tea, the host carefully measures powdered green tea with a bamboo teaspoon, putting the tea into the tea bowl.

8: Using the bamboo dipper, the host pours hot water from the kettle into the tea bowl. He can pour any extra water back into the kettle.

9: The host stirs the tea vigorously with a bamboo whisk until the tea is light and frothy. It is a bright green color.

10: When the host has given the bowl of tea to the guest, they bow to each other before the guest begins to drink the tea.

11: The guest drinks the tea by holding the bowl in the palm of the left hand and guiding it with a flattened right hand.

12: After drinking the tea, the guest places the bowl in front of her and admires it. She may ask the host questions about the bowl.

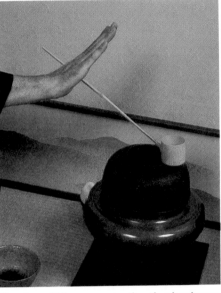

Many beautiful movements other than bowing are a part of the tea ceremony. This gesture is used to put the dipper down after pouring the water.

The Japanese symbols, from left to right, are for harmony, respect, purity, and tranquillity—the four elements of the tea ceremony.

Philip Perl is a writer who was born in Manhattan and educated at Columbia University. He was on the staff of The New Yorker *magazine for 20 years, then became a terrarium specialist and sand painter at Terrarium Town in New York, where he also teaches.*

TERRARIUMS
Little Worlds Under Glass

Is there a place in the woods that you remember from childhood, perhaps an idyllic forest glade briefly glimpsed, a haunting landscape that you now escape to only in fantasies? In a terrarium (a miniature garden under glass) such a place can be recreated and kept alive—even in a sunless city apartment—for contemplation and enjoyment of extraordinary beauty. The idea of a miniature garden is an ancient heritage, dating back to the Greeks who cultivated such gardens under translucent bell jars and offered them to the gods. Romans called them *terraria* and enjoyed them for their novelty and beauty. But the terrarium as it is cultivated today—in a closed environment—is credited to an accidental discovery by a London botanist, Dr. Nathaniel Ward, in the first half of the nineteenth century. Intending to observe the reproductive habits of the moth, the doctor put some earth and an unhatched cocoon into a transparent glass container and sealed it. What he witnessed was the spontaneous growth of plants from seeds and spores already in the soil. The plants thrived for months (some say years) without additional water or any other attention. His Wardian case, as it became known, was quickly adopted as a feature in fashionable Victorian houses where indoor gardening was developing as a fad of the day.

How Terrariums Work
The terrarium, something like a tiny greenhouse, is an efficient system for recycling air and water. The transparent container admits light but, when closed, it lets the moisture in the soil vaporize and condense continuously (Figure A). This gives the plants an almost inexhaustible supply of moisture and carbon dioxide. You can let a terrarium subsist on a tablespoon of water for a month at a time, without harm to the plants, if you are taking a long vacation, or if you just don't feel like fussing. Of course plants, like other living things, thrive best in fresh air; so while the terrarium's environment does not demand renewal, I never leave the plants totally sealed in unless it is necessary.

Materials
Terrariums are easy to make and the materials needed are widely and cheaply available. The container may be of any size as long as there is an opening large enough to put your hand through. (A bottle garden is a kind of terrarium, but its narrow opening forces the use of tongs for planting.) Beverage mugs, fish tanks and bowls, and brandy snifters are all possible terrarium containers. In time, you may want one of the large containers available at terrarium shops. Some are shaped like houses with roofs and chimneys (opposite); others are leaded cylinders with insets of glass. Whatever your choice, the glass or plastic should be colorless or very lightly tinted. Dark glass impedes the passage of light needed to keep the terrarium plants healthy and will prevent you from seeing the plants clearly. In any case, emphasize the contents of the terrarium, not the container itself. The planting medium for all terrariums consists of layers of gravel, charcoal, and soil.

Terrarium Plants
Slow-growing miniature plants are natural choices for a terrarium. Generally, these fall into three categories: tropical, nontropical, and the family of cacti and succulents. To achieve the best results, do not mix plants from different categories in one terrarium. Each group has different temperature and light requirements. In the Craftnotes on page 2456, some plants in each category are listed—with the temperatures they need. This is but a small selection—there are hundreds more. The projects that follow show how to create three distinctly different types of terrariums. In each case, feel free to substitute other plants that you like.

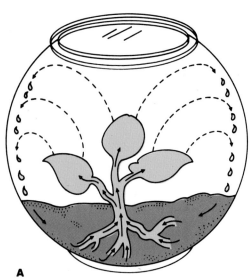

A

Figure A: In a sealed terrarium, moisture can be recycled almost indefinitely. A plant draws water from the soil, then exhales it through its leaves as vapor. The vapor condenses on the container walls and runs back to the soil.

A leaded glass terrarium, landscaped with tree bark and volcanic rocks, simulates a tropical rain forest. Hinged panels in the top pyramids fold out to allow access to the otherwise airtight enclosure. When the terrarium is sealed, plants within remain healthy with just a few drops of water per month. Instructions for making terrariums from common household containers begin on page 2454.

This vest-pocket terrarium in an apothecary jar is planted with two kinds of Swedish ivy (left and right foreground) and an artillery plant (right background). They will soon fill the space.

Greenery and Growing Things
A simple tropical terrarium ¢ ◻ 👫 🐿

A small apothecary jar, like the one at left, makes an excellent container for a first terrarium. It will serve as much for practice as for permanence. (The jar pictured came as a gift, festooned with ribbons and filled with peppermint sticks.)

Before you put anything into a terrarium, be sure the container is scrupulously clean to protect the future health of the plants.

For good drainage, start with a layer of gravel in the bottom of the container (photograph 1). Any of the grades available in pet and plant stores will do. You might even be able to gather your own gravel. Whatever the source, wash it with hot soapy water. The gravel should cover the bottom of the container to a depth of 1 inch. If in doubt, err on the side of generosity; more can only improve the drainage.

Cover the gravel with a thin layer of crushed (but not powdered) charcoal (photograph 2). It is available at any plant store. This will help to keep the terrarium free of unpleasant odors that might result from mildew, poor air circulation, or root rot. The layer of charcoal can also be decorative if you make it thick enough so you can see where it touches the glass. When you add soil, you will have a foundation of white, black, and brown layers beneath the plants.

Adding the Soil

You have two options when you add a 1- to 2-inch layer of soil atop the charcoal. You can buy packaged soil mixture prepared especially for terrariums. You can also buy potting soil and adjust it for terrarium use by adding equal parts of peat moss and washed sand—the kind prepared for use in concrete and mortar (beach sand is too salty and impure). It is not a good idea to use soil from your own yard unless you have a good idea of its composition and are willing to undertake the smelly process of oven sterilization to get rid of insect eggs and weed seeds.

Some people put a piece of nylon screening or nylon stocking between the charcoal and the soil to keep them separated, but I find the nylon can become an impediment to good air and water circulation.

Place the soil mixture on top of the layer of charcoal, sloping it slightly so the front is perhaps an inch lower than the back. Make natural steps in your terrarium using three roughly matching stones, each about an inch long. Place one toward the back of the glass, one in the center, and one near the front (photograph 3). White stones will seem quite prominent against the green moss that will eventually cover the soil; other stone colors will blend nicely with it. As a general rule, avoid any artificially colored gravel or stone. A natural look is best.

Planting

For each plant, make a small hole with the tip of a spoon handle (photograph 4); then press the plant roots gently in place and cover them. The left side of the jar

1: Start with a layer of washed gravel in the bottom of the container to improve the drainage in the terrarium. This is essential since a terrarium has no hole in the bottom.

2: Pour a thin layer of charcoal over the gravel to absorb odors that may develop within the confined growing space.

3: Slope the soil so it is an inch higher at the back than the front; then press three 1-inch stones into place to create natural-looking steps.

4: Make a tiny hole for each plant with the tip of a spoon handle. Place the plant in the hole, and gently press the soil around it.

pictured opposite has been planted with a miniature Swedish ivy (*Plectanthrus Oertendahlii*), its pale-green leaves dappled in cream. On the other side is an artillery plant (*Pilea microphylla*), whose tiny leaves look like clusters of tiny stones, and what is popularly called the mystery plant (*Plectanthrus coleoides marginatus*), another variety of Swedish ivy. These three plants are all that fit comfortably within the jar: their growth will fill the limited space soon enough. Avoid jamming more plants into a space than look comfortable together. The plants will be healthier if they have a little growing space.

Terrarium Care

When the plants seem to be crowding each other or are growing out of the top of the terrarium, don't hesitate to pinch them back, either with your thumb and forefinger or with scissors. Terrarium plants are usually slow growing, but sometimes they burst their bounds. If one of the plants becomes gargantuan and you like it that way, remove it and plant it in a flowerpot. Give its space in the terrarium to a smaller plant. If, on the other hand, one of the plants seems to be in failing health, banish it quickly.

Since terrarium plants are kept small, they need little plant food. But they will in time exhaust the soil's nutrients. Feed your terrarium plants with minuscule amounts of fish emulsion, an organic fertilizer made from fish by-products. Once a month, put a drop in a glass of water, and sprinkle on enough to darken the soil.

Moss

To complete the terrarium, you need a plant material that will give you a thick, velvety ground cover. In a small container, natural moss is a good choice. The amount you need should be easy to find, even in a city. (I am not suggesting that you denude the parks of moss.) You can also buy moss seed in packages; it grows very slowly.

Cut away as much soil as you can from the bottom of the moss. Then fit small pieces of moss carefully around the stems of the plants and between the stones (photograph 5). This is the quickest way to get a green carpet in a terrarium. If it gets enough moisture, the moss will stay green.

There is another way to handle moss that is less attractive and more troublesome at the start. It will give you a richer and hardier growth once the moss becomes established. Again, cut away as much soil as possible from the bottom. Use a knife to chop what is left into the smallest possible bits. Spread the paste that results over the soil in the terrarium; then sprinkle a bit more soil lightly over the chopped moss. In a few weeks, the moss will reestablish itself.

Watering

Shower the terrarium generously when you have finished it. You can see if you have given it enough water by looking at the soil next to the glass. It should be one solid dark color all the way through, with no light area at the bottom. But don't over water: a sure sign is water backing up through the moss. With a little practice and careful observation, you can determine the proper amount of water to add whenever the soil looks dry.

A good terrarium-watering implement is a rubber laundry sprinkler, which will produce a rainy rather than a misty effect. It is particularly good for occasional heavy waterings. A long-nosed watering can is also useful for delivering water directly to the base of each plant, regardless of its proximity to others. A spray mister provides a fine dew that helps if humidity is low, but it will not water the soil deeply (photograph 6) and should be used about once a week.

If you use a container that has a cover, even the metal screw-on kind that comes with food jars, you can leave it on the terrarium and water far less frequently than if you leave the terrarium open. But take the cover off now and then, especially in summer, to keep it from getting so fetid inside that your plants mildew. As long as beads of moisture are clinging to the glass, you don't need to water a covered terrarium. With an open terrarium, check the soil color, and water if it's light.

You can improvise a cover for an open terrarium from a square of window glass fitted over the top. A small glass dish or ashtray could also be used. If you are going on vacation, a sheet of plastic food wrap stretched across the top, with an airhole or two punched in it, will serve as a temporary cover.

This tropical terrarium displays, clockwise from lower left: palm, bloodleaf, and a tropical evergreen seedling.

5: Fit pieces of the moss around the plant stems and the stones, pressing them gently against the soil to form a ground cover.

6: Use a mister (above) to refresh the tiny plants, but use a laundry sprinkler to water the terrarium until the layer of soil is evenly moistened and darkened all the way through.

CRAFTNOTES: TERRARIUM PLANTS AND TEMPERATURES

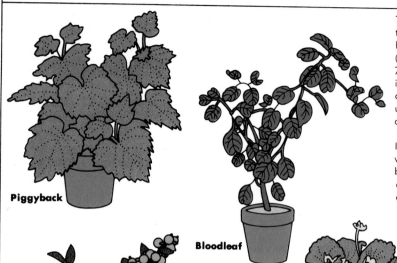

Tropical terrarium plants grow best when the winter temperature is kept above 70 degrees Fahrenheit; nontropicals will be healthier if they are kept in temperatures below 70 degrees (but well above freezing, of course). If your home is around the 70-degree dividing line, you can combine both types of plants in one terrarium, since their moisture and light requirements are for the most part compatible. In homes kept at 70 or above, use only tropicals in the terrarium. If you like your house quite cool in winter, use only nontropicals.

Place your terrarium in bright light but not in direct sunlight. If your room is rather dark even at midday, light the terrarium with 80 watts of fluorescent light or a 75-watt incandescent bulb, suspended 2 to 3 feet above the plants. Keep the lights on at all times except for eight hours at night; the plants need some rest every day.

Piggyback

Bloodleaf

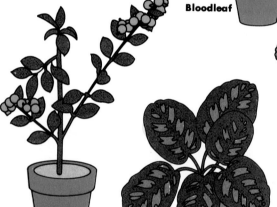

Coral berry

Prayer plant

African violet

Pincushion cactus

Jade plant

Star cactus

Crown-of-thorns

Maidenhair fern

Recommended tropical terrarium plants:
African violet (Saintpaulia)
Aluminum plant (Pilea cadierei)
Artillery plant (Pilea microphylla)
Bloodleaf (Iresine)
Coral-berry (Ardisia crispa)
Creeping fig (Ficus repens)
Dracaena (Dracaena Sanderiana)
Dwarf gloxinia (Sinningia pusilla)
Emerald ripple (Peperomia caperatazo)
English ivy (Hedera helix)
Filigree plant (Fittonia)
Marble wax plant (Peperomia obtusifolia variegata)
Mystery plant (Plectanthrus coleoides marginatus)
Palm (Neanthe bella)
Peacock plant (Calathea)
Pink-polka-dot plant (Hypoestes sanguinolenta)
Prayer plant (Maranta)
Purple heart (Setcreasea purpurea)
Strawberry begonia (Saxifraga sarmentosa)
Swedish ivy (Plectanthrus Oertendahlii)

Some suggested cacti:
Barrel cactus (Parodia aureispina)
Bunny ears (Opuntia microdasys)
Old man (Cephalocereus senilis)
Peanut cactus (Chamaecereus silvestri)
Pincushion (Mammillaria)
Star cactus (Astrophytum)

Some suggested succulents:
Burro's tail (Sedum Morganianum)
Crown-of-thorns (Euphorbia splendens)
Elephant bush (Portulacaria afra variegata)
Hen-and-chicks (Sempervivum soboliferum)
Jade plant (Crassula portulacea)
Living stone (Lithops)
Snake plant (Sanseviera hahnii)

Recommended nontropical terrarium plants include:
Asparagus fern (Asparagus plumosus)
Beauty fern (Pteris ensiformis Victoriae)
Bird's nest fern (Asplenium nidus)
Brake fern (Pellaea rotundifolia)
Club moss (Selaginella Kraussiana brownii)
Fluffy ruffles fern (Nephrolepis exaltata)
Maidenhair fern (Adiantum bellum)
Partridgeberry (Mitchella repens)
Panamanian love plant (Pellionia)
Piggyback plant (Tolmiea menziesii)
Pipsissewa (Chimaphila umbellata)
Rabbit's-foot-fern (Davallia)
Touch-me-not (Mimosa pudica)

A woodland dell is created in a goldfish bowl with the lush growth of several kinds of ferns. Granite cliffs simulated with bark, a brook made of pebbles, and a footbridge of lashed toothpicks add to the landscape in a tiny, self-sufficient environment.

Greenery and Growing Things

A fern terrarium (nontropical) $ 🗌 👫 ☕

In a medium-sized goldfish bowl, 10 inches in diameter, you can create a glen of ferns, complete with a simulated brook and bridge. If you don't have such a bowl, it is easy to find one at a variety store. A globe is a pleasing shape for a terrarium, since with the plants inside it suggests a miniature planet.

The first steps in planting the globe are the same as those described for an apothecary jar (page 2454). You need a layer of gravel, one of charcoal, and one of soil. But, instead of simply sloping the soil from back to front, this time you should pile it much higher at the back, to suggest a bluff across the middle of the

Beauty ferns at left, table ferns in the rear, maidenhair fern at right center, and fluffy ruffles in the right foreground fill this lush forest floor. The green shoot nestled in the rock at left is a bird's-nest fern.

terrarium. This bluff will be held with tree bark, with a mottled silvery-brown surface to suggest a granite palisade. Strip the bark from a dry piece of firewood. Segments measuring 2 by 5 and 3 by 5 inches are all you will need. Spray the bark with insecticide to eliminate any unwelcome tenants.

Position the bark vertically in the soil, one end of each piece touching the glass on either side, the other ends not quite touching in the center (photograph 7). Fill in additional soil behind the top edge. This will give you two planting levels. The place where the bark pieces meet will be the source of a cataract, simulated with pebbles, that plunges to the lower level.

A Choice of Ferns

Plant the upper level with an assortment of ferns, not more than half-a-dozen in all. For a sampling from the almost limitless world of ferns, I choose the following: beauty fern (*Pteris ensiformis Victoriae*), with notched leaves delicately bordered in white; fluffy ruffles (*Nephrolepis exaltata*), with finely crinkled and abundant leaves; bird's nest fern (*Asplenium nidus*), with spikey, closely packed leaves that look more like a pineapple top than a bird's nest; asparagus fern (*Asparagus plumosus*), not really a fern but a plant that looks and behaves like one, with fronds so ethereal they appear to have been sketched with a pen running out of ink; and finally my own favorite, a maidenhair fern (*Adiantum bellum*), with cloverlike

7: Two pieces of bark set into the soil simulate a granite cliff. Fill in the back of the container with more soil at a higher level.

8: A Maidenhair Fern planted on the top level of the terrarium will suggest a majestic tree at the top of the cliff.

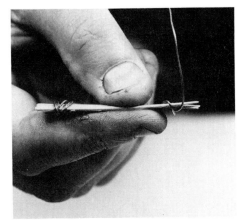

9: Simulate a mountain stream by sprinkling white gravel in a depression between the two pieces of bark, from top to bottom.

10: To make a miniature bridge, bind three or four toothpicks together at the ends, keeping them flat between thumb and forefinger.

11: Gently set the toothpick bridge in place across the stream, anchoring it with a small stone if necessary.

leaves, pale green suffused in paler pink, floating on delicate black stems (photograph 8). If you have a favorite fern, by all means include it.

Next, take a spoonful of the same kind of gravel that you used in the bottom layer and trickle it from back to front of the lower level, as yet unplanted (photograph 9). This is meant to suggest a mountain stream; make it as wide or as narrow as you like. To make the stream seem to come rushing down from the heights above, press the soil between the two pieces of bark with your finger to less than a 45-degree angle and fill that trough with the same kind of gravel.

The lower level beside the stream can be planted with more ferns, or, if you like contrast, with Panamanian love plant (*Pellionia*) which has delicate green tracings on its brown leaves and touch-me-not (*Mimosa pudica*), a sensitive plant whose tiny oval leaves cling to each other. Harder to find, but worth seeking, is partridgeberry (*Mitchella repens*) a tiny woods plant that will provide a spot of bright red color when it bears fruit.

To complete the terrarium, cover the exposed soil. You can do this with moss (page 2455) or use a ground cover such as baby's tears (*Helxine soleirolii*) or miniature club moss (*Selaginella Kraussiana brownii*). Clumps of either spread rapidly with good humidity. (I have always been cautioned to cut baby's tears with scissors, and never to pull it apart by hand.)

As a final touch, link the two banks of the stream with a wooden bridge, made by lashing six toothpicks together with bits of wire or floral tape (photograph 10). Hold the toothpicks flat between thumb and forefinger while lashing them so they do not bunch up. Place the finished bridge across the gravel stream (photograph 11). Water the glen until all the soil is darkened and the terrarium is finished.

A rectangular tank, edged with redwood strips, is the setting for a collection of tiny cacti and succulents. Because these denizens of the desert require little water, the container is never covered.

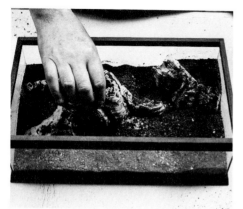

12: Pieces of bark set vertically into the soil of a desert terrarium appear to be jagged rock out-croppings.

Greenery and Growing Things
A cactus terrarium

A desert terrarium, stark and sere, provides a dramatic miniature landscape. The one shown above is housed in a rectangular container handsomely edged with redwood strips. If you do not want to buy a special terrarium like this, you could duplicate the scene in a rectangular fish tank.

This desert terrarium is virtually carefree, even though it is open on top. It needs watering only once a month in winter and once every other week in summer. It will not need feeding for years if you add a tablespoonful of bonemeal to the soil mixture to serve as cacti fertilizer.

To make your own planting medium, use one part potting soil, one part peat moss, two parts sand, and one part perlite. Or buy cactus soil already mixed.

This terrarium houses both cacti and succulents (cacti have spines; succulents do not). The initial steps in making it are as described on page 2454—a layer of gravel, a layer of charcoal, then a layer of soil rising gradually from front to back. Divide the soil area into several levels with pieces of bark, as described on page 2458, to suggest rock outcroppings (photograph 12). In dry soil, these can easily be moved around to suit your needs as you fill the landscape with plants.

All the cacti used should be miniatures. There is an enormous variety of tiny cacti available—so many that you should never have to plant the same kind twice. In the terrarium above, half a dozen varieties, commonly sold in plant stores, were used.

13: A starlike succulent, hen-and-chickens, looks at home on the lower level of the arid terrain.

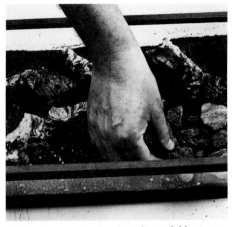

14: Small pieces of volcanic rock, available at garden stores, add to the scene's starkness.

15: A stately three-eared bunny-ears cactus is placed on a hilltop to dominate the landscape.

Front and center in the terrarium, plant six tiny *Sempervivum soboliferum*, the familiar hen-and-chickens beloved of rock gardeners. Set them in two very ragged rows (photograph 13). One thing you don't want is a formal-looking garden in any kind of terrarium.

Form a hill of soil in the right front corner of the tank, and on it, plant one or two miniature barrel cacti (*Parodia aureispina*) or peanut cacti (*Chamaecereus silvestri*). Cacti are extremely shallow-rooted, so you will have to pack the soil in around them to be sure they won't topple when they are watered or moved. Litter the hillside with small chunks of volcanic rock; then press them firmly into the soil. (photograph 14). The result should look as though a glacier deposited the rocks on that hillside. Volcanic rock, also known as lava rock or feather rock, is available at plant supply stores. If you can't find it, use any small irregular stones.

Make Several Levels

Behind a piece of bark on the left side of the tank, plant more miniature barrel cacti. Behind and above them, place another piece of bark, and a few more cacti. In the center, use bark to create as many levels as possible, perhaps three or four in all, and fill the spaces with stately tree cacti (*Cereus peruvianus*). This is a miniature variety of the giant night-blooming cereus, whose fragrantly beautiful flowers are said to drive lovers mad.

Place a large piece of bark diagonally across the right rear corner of the tank. Fill the space behind with soil, and plant one or two bunny ears (*Opuntia microdasys*). The one in photograph 15 has three rabbitlike ears rather than two. *Opuntia* frequently seems two-dimensional, like an angelfish, so let the wide side face front.

To the left of the hen-and-chickens, use a miniature cactus that will contrast with them. My choice was an old-man cactus (*Cephalocereus senilis*), 2 inches high and covered with woolly white hairs. (I have a 2-foot-high old-man cactus, with hairs that can actually be combed.) The white hairs that stand out dramatically against the earth tones of the background and the green of other cacti conceal sharp thorns, so handle with care.

Dry Gulches

Run a trail of white gravel down from the central heights and along the volcanic rocks at the lower right. The effect here, because of the aridity of the landscape, will be that of a dry gulch. Then trickle a bit of sand over the soil (photograph 16) to suggest the shadings that occur naturally in a desert.

A cactus terrarium is always open. The plants will not tolerate the humid atmosphere of a closed container. Cacti in a terrarium must be watered sparingly in any event. Stop watering when the soil against the sides of the tank looks darker than when dry but before it gets soggy; water again when it looks and feels dry.

Place the completed terrarium where it will receive bright light for several hours a day. Apart from infrequent watering, it will need no further attention.

For related projects see "Bottle Gardens" and "Vivariums."

16: Sand sprinkled at random over the planting medium suggests shadings that would naturally occur in a desert.

A cactus terrarium features clockwise from bottom left: round pincushion cactus, jade plant in the background, peanut cactus in the center, slender spikey cereus to the right, and in the foreground, a star-shaped gold-tooth aloe.

2461

TERRINES AND TIMBALES
Continental Casseroles

Fran Shinagel (far left) has a love of cooking that was nurtured in the kitchen of her Neapolitan grandmother. A free-lance fashion consultant, she cooks for an appreciative family—her husband and two daughters, Eva and Nina. Terrines are one of her specialties, but she is adept at many cuisines.

Anna-Teresa Callen (left) shares her quick-and-easy recipes for delicately flavored timbales, casseroles that make the most of almost any food. Born in Pescara, Italy, on the Adriatic, she acquired her cooking skills by watching good cooks at work when she was a child. Anna-Teresa balances New York careers as a television researcher and manager of an art gallery with a busy social life.

Terrines and timbales are casserole meals with a continental accent. Though both are celebrated French dishes, cooks of almost every cuisine have their own versions which they have created to please their own tastes. The terrine, a meat dish something like a meat loaf, is named for the oval dish of glazed earthenware in which it is traditionally cooked. It is sliced and served cold, and can be as simple as the one-meat liver pâté on page 2464—perfect picnic fare—or as elaborate as the festive dish opposite and on page 2466 that combines several kinds of meats, other ingredients, and spices.

A timbale, named for an Arabian kettledrum, is a dish usually cooked in a tin mold, either a large ring mold or small individual ones. This delicate dish is baked, then is usually unmolded and served hot, with a sauce. It can be an elegant main dish or, baked in small molds, an individual side dish accompanying the entrée. A timbale is easy to prepare and can incorporate a great variety of ingredients—meat, fish, vegetables, or combinations thereof—making it an excellent way to transform leftovers into haute cuisine.

Utensils

To make terrines and timbales, you need a blender; in both cases part or all of the mixture must be puréed. In addition, some meats for terrines must be ground in a meat grinder. Traditionally, terrines are baked in glazed earthenware casseroles but you can use porcelain, enameled iron, or ovenproof glassware instead. If you do not have a tin ring mold in which to make a timbale, substitute individual ones such as those shown in photographs 15 and 16, page 2469. Other essential utensils include measuring spoons, measuring cups, sharp knives for chopping and slicing, wooden mixing spoons in various sizes, and a rubber spatula.

Room for Experiments

If you are just learning to cook, you should know that the best chefs agree that a good cook is someone who can make the best of whatever ingredients are available, someone who is continually experimenting with foods and flavors, cultivating a sense of taste and learning how to combine ingredients. Underlying all is an interest in food and a love of preparing delicious meals and sharing them with an appreciative audience. For beginning and experienced cooks alike, one-dish meals like terrines and timbales allow a lot of room for experimenting with ingredients, techniques, and flavors. Note that a recipe is not necessarily difficult because it has a long list of ingredients, as in *Terrine à la Francesca* (page 2466). Moreover, the dish is worth the extra preparation time required. A little extra care goes a long way; the proof is in the eating.

A terrine is an elegant casserole: five kinds of meat and many spices went into the one pictured opposite. The recipe (page 2466) may seem difficult because it has a long list of ingredients, but it takes time rather than culinary skill to create.

Panade

Panade, a thickening mixture for the pâté, is rice cooked in bouillon until very soft.

Ingredients:

⅓ cup rice
1 cup water, beef broth, or bouillon
3 tablespoons butter

Combine all panade ingredients in a saucepan, and cook over high heat for about 25 minutes, or until very soft.

1: The first step in making a liver pâté is to cube the liver that will be puréed in a blender.

2: Panade, a thickening mixture, is rice cooked very soft in bouillon. It is added to the puréed liver mixture in the blender.

$ ▯ ♟ ♨

Liver terrine or pâté (serves ten as appetizer)

Any kind of liver can be used to make this simple terrine: pork, calf, beef, or, of course, goose liver, the basis for the most famous of all pâtés, *pâté de foie gras*. A pâté served with fresh bread and wine makes a delicious lunch.

Ingredients:

½ pound liver
½ pound pork fat cubed
½ to ¾ pound pork fat sliced thin for lining the terrine
¾ to 1 cup panade (left)
1 egg
1 tablespoon cognac or bourbon
2½ teaspoons salt
1 large pinch of each: pepper, allspice, and nutmeg
Minced truffles (optional)
Bay leaf
Sprinkling of thyme

Preheat the oven to 350 degrees Fahrenheit. Cube the liver (photograph 1); then purée it in the blender, adding the egg and all the seasonings except the bay leaf and thyme. Add the panade to the blender (photograph 2). Dice the pork fat (photograph 3) and add it to the mixture. Blend well. If the blender stalls, turn it off and push the mixture down with a spatula (photograph 4). Fry a small amount of the mixture and taste for seasoning (photograph 5). Line a dish with thinly sliced pork fat (photograph 6) and pour in the mixture (photograph 7). Cover the mixture completely with the fat (photograph 8); then put the bay leaf and a sprinkling of thyme on top. Cover with a double thickness of aluminum foil and add the lid if the baking dish has one. Place the dish in a roasting pan and pour boiling water into the pan (photograph 9) until the water comes two-thirds of the way up the side of the dish. Bake 1½ hours at 350 degrees Fahrenheit. Remove from the oven, empty the remaining water, then place the terrine back in the roasting pan. Weight the terrine to compress the meat as it cools (photograph 10), and let it cool to room temperature (this will take about six hours). Then refrigerate it for at least ten hours without removing the weight. This terrine will keep up to ten days, and the flavor improves with age. To serve, unmold the terrine by holding it upside down, uncovered, under warm running water. Have one hand ready to catch it as it slips out. Do not remove the fat. Serve as shown in photograph 11, and sliced, below.

Slices of liver pâté are served with their pork-fat rind, which is removed before the pâté is eaten. Fresh French bread and wine complement the dish.

3: Dice the pork fat into ¼-inch pieces and add it to the puréed liver mixture in the blender.

4: If the mixture clogs the blender blades, turn off the machine and push the mixture down, loosening it gently with a rubber spatula.

5: Test-fry a small portion of the mixture so you can taste it to check the seasoning. *Never taste an uncooked meat mixture.*

6: Line the baking dish with thin slices of pork fat, letting strips overhang the sides so you will be able to cover the top.

7: Pour the mixture that you have blended into the lined dish. (For Terrine à la Francesca, page 2466, half-fill the dish, then lay in the chicken breasts.)

8: Cover the mixture completely by folding in the overhanging strips of pork fat; then sprinkle with thyme and place a bay leaf on top.

9: Cover the dish tightly with foil; then set it in a pan and pour enough boiling water around it to cover the bottom two-thirds of the baking dish.

10: After you remove the cooked terrine from the oven, empty any remaining water. Place heavy weights on top of the meat to compress it further.

11: After refrigeration, the unmolded terrine is ready to be served in its blanket of pork fat. Slice with a sharp knife.

12: To start a five-meat terrine, cut two skinned chicken breasts into four equal parts, as shown.

13: Wrap each piece of chicken breast that you have space for in pork fat. Set one or two pieces lengthwise in a terrine half-filled with a ground-meat mixture (photograph 7). Then pour the remaining mixture over to cover. Cover the loaf in pork fat as shown in photograph 8.

Ingredients:

2½ pounds fresh pork fat (1 pound sliced thin to line each 3-cup terrine). It is better to buy more than you think you will need, for any excess can be frozen.
½ pound boneless veal
½ pound boneless pork shoulder
¼ pound ham in one piece
¼ pound tongue in one piece
1 chicken breast (2 halves) boned and skinned
½ pound calf or beef liver
2 tablespoons heavy cream
2 eggs
¼ cup cognac or bourbon
¼ cup chopped truffles and juice, canned (optional)
6 tablespoons flour
Salt and pepper to taste
½ teaspoon allspice
¼ teaspoon cinnamon
½ teaspoon ground cloves (or to taste)
1 or 2 large bay leaves
Large pinch of thyme for each terrine

A classic terrine is baked in an oval crock of glazed earthenware. The one above, with a sprig of thyme nestled in the pure white fat, is ready to unmold and serve. The recipe is below.

Terrine à la Francesca

This recipe makes 6 cups for one 6-cup terrine or two 3-cup terrines, and serves 8 to 10 people. Ingredients are listed at left.

Preheat the oven to 400 degrees Fahrenheit. Cube the liver and purée it with the eggs and cognac in the blender. The mixture should be soupy and smooth. Add another egg or a little cream if the mixture seems too dry. If the chunks of meat are thick, the blender may clog. In this case, add more cream. Add the seasonings and the flour, except the bay leaf and thyme; then blend and pour into a large bowl.

Cube and mix ¼ pound of pork, ¼ pound of veal, ¼ pound of pork fat, ⅛ pound of ham, and ⅛ pound of tongue. Put the mixture through a meat grinder three times, using the fine blade.

Dice the remaining meats and fat (except the chicken breasts) in ¼-inch cubes. Add this and the ground meat to the puréed mixture in the bowl and mix well. Fry a spoonful of the mixture, taste it, and adjust the seasonings if necessary.

Slice the breast of chicken into four equal pieces (photograph 12) and wrap each in one slice of pork fat (photograph 13). Line the terrine with pork fat (photograph 6, page 2465), overlapping the edges all around.

Half-fill the lined terrine with the meat mixture. Put in one or two wrapped chicken breasts lengthwise, pour in the remaining filling; then fold over the pork fat strips, completely enclosing the filling. Put a bay leaf and a sprinkling of thyme on top. Tightly cover the terrine with a double thickness of aluminum foil; then place the terrine lid on top.

Put the terrine in a roasting pan. Pour boiling water into the pan until it covers two-thirds of the terrine. Cook for three hours at 400 degrees Fahrenheit.

When done, remove the terrine from the oven and empty the remaining water from the pan. Leave the terrine in the pan, but remove the lid and weight the top (photograph 10, page 2465), preferably with something about the same size as the dish. This compresses the meat and will facilitate slicing. Leave the weight in place while the meat cools to room temperature; then refrigerate with the weight still on for 10 or 12 hours. The flavor continues to improve for two or three days; the terrine will keep for a week or ten days.

Unmold the terrine and serve it in thick slices arranged on a platter, as shown on page 2463. Decorate with parsley, and serve with fresh French bread, dry white wine, fruits, and cheese.

Kitchen Favorites and Celebrations
Timbales

In French, it is *timbale*, in Italian *sformato*, but in either case the result is a tasty variation on a casserole. The recipes that follow for chicken, fish, and vegetable timbales may inspire you to invent your own variations. Ingredients for Chicken Timbale are listed at right.

First prepare the Béchamel Sauce. Melt two tablespoons of butter in a saucepan over very low heat. Add the flour gradually, stirring constantly with a wire whisk or wooden spoon. Cook for two or three minutes; then remove the pan from the heat and add the milk slowly, stirring the mixture until it is well blended. Return the pan to the heat and cook over moderate heat, stirring constantly until the sauce is smooth and bubbly. Remove the pan from the heat, season to taste, and set aside.

Sauté the chopped onions very slowly in butter until they are translucent but not browned. Put them in a chopping bowl and add chicken, ham or prosciutto, noodles, and mushrooms. Finely chop all ingredients or put the mixture in the blender and purée it. To this mixture, add Béchamel Sauce, egg yolks (lightly beaten), Swiss cheese, and parsley. Beat the egg whites until they are stiff, and fold them gently into the mixture.

Butter a four-cup ring mold and pour the mixture into it. Set the mold in a shallow pan of boiling water and bake the timbale in a moderate oven (325 degrees Fahrenheit) for 45 to 50 minutes. To test for doneness, insert a toothpick or knife blade into the timbale. If it comes out clean, remove the timbale from the oven; otherwise bake it for five minutes more and test again.

When the timbale is done, run a spatula or knife along the edges of the mold; then invert it on a warm platter. Before serving, make a second batch of Béchamel Sauce, flavored to your taste (variations, page 2468). Pour the sauce over the timbale or serve it on the side.

Chicken Timbale (serves six)

Ingredients:
¾ cup chopped onions
1½ tablespoons butter
1 cup cooked chicken breast, diced
2 slices cooked ham or prosciutto
1 cup cooked noodles (any kind)
6 medium mushrooms, quartered
1 cup Béchamel Sauce
3 eggs, separated into yolks and whites
½ cup grated Swiss cheese
½ cup chopped parsley
Salt and pepper to taste

Béchamel sauce:
2 tablespoons butter
3 tablespoons flour
1¼ cups hot milk
Salt and pepper to taste

Timbales are versatile casserole dishes that can be made with vegetables, meat, or fish.

Bay Scallops Timbale (serves six)
Ingredients:

¾ cup chopped onions
1½ tablespoons butter
1 pound cooked scallops
1 cup cooked rice
3 eggs

½ cup grated Swiss cheese
½ cup parsley
2 tablespoons Marsala or sherry wine
Béchamel Sauce (page 2467) and Mornay
  Sauce (below)
Salt and pepper to taste

Prepare the Béchamel Sauce as for Chicken Timbale. Preheat the oven to 350 degrees Fahrenheit. Place onion, scallops, rice, eggs, cheese, parsley, and seasonings in a blender. Blend at medium speed for two or three minutes, until the mixture is chopped but not finely chopped. Add the prepared Béchamel Sauce and the wine and blend until well mixed. Butter the inside of a six-cup ring mold or individual molds and fill with the mixture to ⅛ inch below the rim.

Bake in a pan of boiling water, as for Chicken Timbale, for 40 to 45 minutes. Test for doneness by inserting a toothpick. To serve, run a knife around the edges, and invert onto a serving platter. Serve with Mornay Sauce.

Mornay Sauce

Prepare the Béchamel Sauce (page 2467) and add to it a pinch of nutmeg and ¼ cup of grated Parmesan cheese or ½ cup of grated Swiss cheese, or a mixture of both.

Aurore Sauce

To the basic Béchamel Sauce, add 2 tablespoons of tomato sauce and a pinch of basil or tarragon.

A timbale can be an elegant addition to a gourmet table, as is this one made with scallops and served with a rich Mornay Sauce. The recipe is above.

Mixed Vegetable Timbale (serves six)

Any number of vegetables, fresh or leftover, may be combined in this timbale version that can be served as a side dish or an entrée. Color is important in giving food an appetizing appearance; green vegetables such as spinach, broccoli, or zucchini always seem to produce good eye appeal.

Ingredients:

6 slices of bacon, crisply cooked
  and crumbled
1 cup fresh bread crumbs
1 cup chicken stock
½ cup milk
3 tablespoons tomato sauce
1 teaspoon tomato paste

2 tablespoons melted butter
1 tablespoon chopped parsley
2 cups mixed vegetables
2 cups boiled or baked potato
3 eggs well beaten
1 pinch oregano, basil, or a mixture of both
Salt and pepper to taste

Preheat the oven to 350 degrees Fahrenheit. Combine bacon with bread crumbs, chicken stock, milk, tomato sauce and paste, butter, parsley, and seasonings. Put vegetables in a blender, first sautéing them if they are fresh. Add eggs one at a time and blend at medium speed until the mixture is quite smooth. Combine this blend with the ingredients previously combined and stir until well mixed (photograph 14). Spoon into well-buttered individual molds (photograph 15) or a large ring mold, and set in a pan of boiling water (photograph 16). Bake in a moderate oven for one hour. Individual timbales can be served around a roast or a baked fish.

For related entries, see "Herbs" and "Pasta."

14: Combine the puréed vegetables from the blender with the bread-crumb mixture, and stir until they are well blended.

15: Fill well-buttered individual molds (or a large ring mold) with the timbale mixture. Do not fill any mold to the top.

16: Put timbales, like terrines, in a pan of boiling water, and bake in the oven until they are done.

To serve individual vegetable timbales, unmold them, cover them with creamy Béchamel Sauce, and garnish with parsley.

TIE DYEING
Tying up a Rainbow

Brant Richardson and some of his friends at nursery school tie-dyed the hand puppets shown in the Craftnotes on page 2475.

When Will and Eileen Richardson collaborated on staging a tie-dye display for a gallery opening, the results were so spectacular they were engaged as tie-dye consultants by fashion designers and the Rit Dye Company. Using the name Up Tied, they created tie-dye designs that won such honors as The Coty Fashion Award and The Vogue American Fabric Award. Their tie dyes have been shown at the Museum of Contemporary Crafts in New York, and examples of their work are part of a worldwide traveling craft show sponsored by the Smithsonian Institution. The Richardsons live in Santa Barbara, California.

The African, Indian, and Japanese words, *adire*, *bandhana*, and *shibori*, meaning to tie and dye, have been used for centuries. The words describe a method of fabric design that is called tie dyeing. In this process, parts of a piece of fabric are pulled into tufts which are bound with string or elastic bands. The material is then saturated with dye. Where the fabric is bound, it resists the dye; elsewhere, the dye is absorbed. Thus patterns like the one pictured opposite and on the following pages are formed. Tie dyeing is one method of resist dyeing. In other methods, wax, wood blocks, or stitches are used to resist the dye. The principle is the same: where the resist is put on the fabric, the fabric does not take the dye.

Resist dyeing originated in the Far East, possibly as early as 3000 B.C. The Romans, among the first to import Eastern fabrics, were mystified by how the gossamer-fine cottons of India and the whispering silks of China were colored.

Although resist dyeing seemed baffling, in time it came to be used in countries as far apart as China and Peru. Many experts believe that tie dyeing was discovered independently in various parts of the world. In India, China, Japan, South America, and Africa, villagers still set aside a special area for fabric dyeing. There, the village dyers congregate, surrounded by dye vats--some 8 feet square--filled with dyes in brilliant hues. Bundles of fabric, dyed and rinsed in river waters, are laid out to dry. Some fabrics are tied and dyed up to eight times, depending on the complexity of the pattern. The care that goes into traditional designs can be bewildering to one accustomed to mass production.

Although resist dyeing can be complex, the basics are easy to master. The projects that follow introduce tie dyeing in single colors, multiple hues, and designs that range from flowing patterns to precise ones. In addition to tie dyeing, tritik (stitch dyeing) and block dyeing are described. Batik, the other major method of resist dyeing, in which melted wax is used, is described elsewhere in this series.

Materials
The materials needed for tie dyeing are: liquid detergent; elastic bands or waxed cord, available at variety stores or stationery shops; squeeze-bottle applicators; liquid or powdered dye in colors of your choice; sponge; rubber gloves; iron; a plastic shower curtain; the fabric to be dyed; and a large enamel, glass, or stainless steel pot. In most cases the pot should be large enough to hold sufficient dye to cover the fabric and allow stirring. If your water has minerals in it, you will also need water softener. Fabrics recommended for dyeing include unbleached muslin, rayon, nylon, acetate, rayon velvet, viscose rayon, linen, burlap, and cotton--but almost any fabric can be tie dyed. Other materials needed in particular types of tie dyeing are listed in instructions for the projects that follow.

Eileen Richardson used fold-dyeing techniques similar to those described on page 2484 to make this wall hanging, *The Black Star*. This is a replica of the original design that won the Vogue Fabric Award in 1970 and is part of the permanent collection at the Metropolitan Museum of Art in New York. Eileen spent three months blending dyes and knotting folded silk squares until she achieved a black dye that would bleed orange and olive green, but when placed in color remover, would turn a rosy pink.

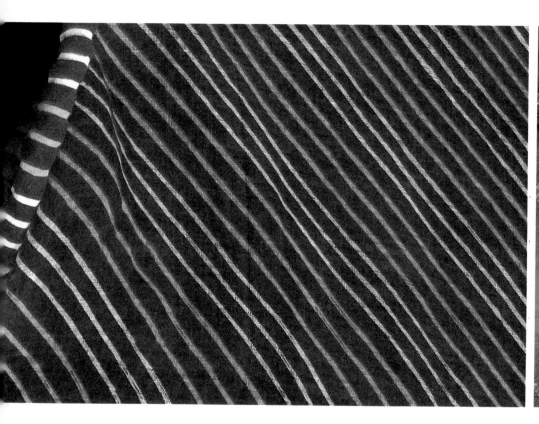

Above: In India, fine fabrics such as this piece of cotton are rolled on the bias and tied tightly with string, spaced at regular intervals. The white cloth is dyed in a light-color dye, then more sections are tied, then the cloth is dipped in a darker dyebath. The result is a design of multicolored stripes known as *Laharya*.

Above (center): In Japan, it is traditional to stitch intricate patterns like these into silk, which is then gathered before it is immersed in the dyebath. This detail is from a stitch-dyed quilt made in Kyoto.

Above (opposite page): African tie-dye designs such as this one from Ghana are brilliantly colored with natural dyes. This design seems to incorporate both the doughnut knots and the stripe folds described on page 2474.

Basic Tie Dyeing

Several tie-dyeing methods are used in the projects that follow. In some cases, liquid dye is squeezed onto specific portions of a fabric that will be knotted, or dye is poured on tied areas. Powdered dye can be prepared in a bath in which the tied fabric is fully immersed. Sometimes tied knots float on the surface of the dyebath.

For consistent results, the fabric must be damp when it is tied and when it is dyed. (This is especially important when you pour colors directly onto the fabric.) Before dyeing, all fabrics should be washed in hot, soapy water to remove the sizing. Most fabrics should then be rinsed to remove the soap; the exceptions are permanent press, waterproof, and rayon-velvet fabrics. These should be soaked in hot water and detergent but not rinsed, as the soap film helps the fabrics absorb the dye evenly. After you have washed the fabric, wring it out and knot it while it is still damp. If you are applying dye directly to the fabric, use a squeeze-bottle applicator or an eyedropper to control the dye. Liquid household dye, undiluted, is recommended for this, but you can use powdered dye mixed with water instead. In any case, shake the dye mixture well, and mix warm water with the dye to help it penetrate the fabric. Whether or not you have applied dye directly to the fabric, wet the fabric before you put it into the dyebath to heighten the resist for best results.

To prepare the dyebath, calculate how big a pot you need to accommodate the fabric. For even dyeing, the pot should be large enough to hold the tied fabric without crowding. Fill the pot with hot water; then add the dye. The instructions on the dye package apply to even dyeing of fabric, not to tie dyeing. It is easier to get even coloring with dark dyes. Light dyes can be diluted with water to promote even dyeing. Bring the dyebath to a simmer, and keep it at that heat throughout the dyeing process. This will produce washfast colors.

Immerse the fabric in the simmering dyebath, keeping the fabric covered. Stir frequently to promote even coloring. How long the fabric should remain in the dyebath depends on the material you are using and how intense you want the color to be. In general, 30 minutes to an hour is sufficient. If you are working with a fabric such as acetate, which wrinkles permanently at a high temperature, keep the dyebath lower than simmer and dye the fabric longer. See "Color Controls," opposite, for additional information.

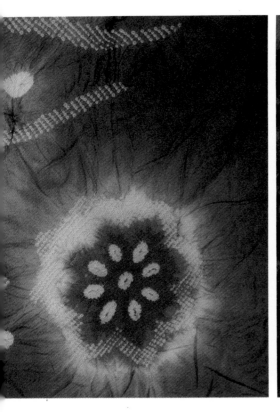

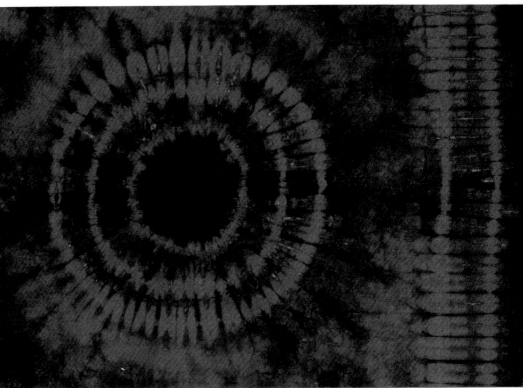

After the fabric has soaked for the required time, remove it from the pot. Without removing bands, clamps, blocks, or other resist materials, rinse the fabric under cool running water until all excess dye has been washed away. When the water runs clear, the dye will not stain other fabrics. Then remove the resist materials and rinse the fabric once more, again until the water runs clear. Rinse and untie each color separately. Hang up the fabric, but keep it out of direct sunlight as it dries; put plastic on the floor under it to avoid stains. You can use the spin cycle on your washing machine to remove excess moisture, but clean the machine by running it through a complete wash cycle with bleach and detergent before you launder in it. Hand launder tie-dyed garments several times, or machine wash them separately in cool water, before you wash them with other clothes.

Color Controls

The color of the cloth you start with affects the colors of the finished design. The lighter the cloth, the more colors you can produce with dyes. For your first tie-dyeing experiments, use household dyes and compatible fabrics, as suggested at right. When you use more than one color, start with the lightest and end with the darkest unless otherwise specified in the directions. A dark color dyed over a light one produces a third color, but a light color over a dark tends to disappear. To economize on dyes, use three primary colors—pinkish red, yellow, and blue—to make other colors. Mixtures of pink and blue produce purple; pink and yellow yield orange; yellow and blue make green.

To lighten a dark color such as navy or brown, leave the fabric in the dyebath for a shorter time than specified, or soak the fabric in a weaker dyebath. To darken a color, use a more concentrated dyebath for a longer time.

Colors always look lighter when dry than when wet. Before you unknot a piece of cloth, iron an edge of the fabric until it is dry. If the color is too light, return the fabric to the dyebath, adding dye to the pot to strengthen the mixture. (But never add dye when the fabric is in the pot.) If the color is too intense, heat a pot of clear water, add a teaspoon of detergent, and simmer the fabric until the water changes color. To change a color in midstream, simmer the knotted fabric in color remover, available where dyes are sold. Do not use bleach. Wash the fabric in hot, soapy water, rinse it, and redye the cloth to the desired color without removing the knots.

Tie dyes

Household dyes are recommended for beginners. They are safe and easy to use on almost all fabrics except Orlon acrylic, some polyesters, other acrylics, and Fiberglas. (Some nylon fibers, too, such as Quiana, will not take dye.) Household dyes are brightest (in descending order) on cotton, silk, nylon, rayon, acetate, and wool. One package of household dye will color one pound (about 3 yards) of a medium-weight fabric. Store mixed household dyes in sealed jars for future use.

To dye a pattern on a piece of cloth, you will need to tie off specific areas so they resist dye. The most popular knots and folds are shown below. The drawing shows how each is made; the photograph shows the pattern-test results. By fastening elastic bands, thread, or wood blocks on the cloth, you can create designs such as sunbursts and stripes. To familiarize yourself with these techniques, practice on an old cotton sheet. (You might like to practice these knots and folds on a hand puppet, as shown opposite. Enlarge two copies of the puppet design shown on tracing paper. Lay both on cotton fabric. Cut out both patterns and use whip or running stitches to seam the edges, except the opening for your hand.)

Rosette knot: To make a circle, pull up a tuft of fabric. Close it tightly at the bottom with an elastic band. The diameter of the circle will be twice the height of the raised area.

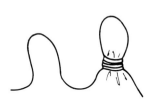

Windup rosette knot: To make a sunburst, begin the same way you would start a rosette. Bind the base; then tightly wrap an elastic band up the stem using a random spiral motion. By using additional bands you can create a more intricate pattern.

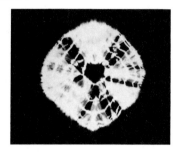

Doughnut (double rosette): To make a pattern of concentric circles, raise a section of the fabric as for a rosette. Hold the base with your thumb and forefinger as you push the top of the raised section back through to the other side; then put on the elastic band.

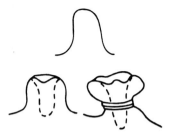

Stripe: To make a stripe, use a ruler and chalk to draw a guideline on the cloth. Neatly pleat the fabric accordian-style along the line. With elastic bands, tightly bind the cloth on the line. For multiple stripes, draw several guidelines. For broad stripes, cover a wider area with bands.

Double stripe: To manage cumbersome lengths of fabric or to achieve soft irregular stripes, pleat the fabric as described below for the regular stripe. But fold the fabric over on itself before tying.

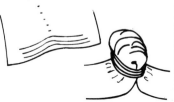

Puckering: A soft marbleized effect can be achieved by pinching the fabric into puckers of varying lengths with one hand while you hold them in place with the other. Bind the fabric just tightly enough to hold the puckers in place. White blotches will result if the elastic bands are too tight. To dye fabric knotted this way, submerge the fabric below the bands in a shallow pan holding ½ to 2 inches of dye. Pour additional colors into the knots on top to heat set as the bottom is dyeing.

Bunching: This knot is excellent for coloring small areas where a haphazard pattern is acceptable. It is fast and easy, but not always controllable. You just wad or scrunch the fabric into a lump and wrap it with elastic bands. The tighter the bands or the wetter the fabric, the less the color from the main dyebath will penetrate.

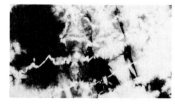

Tied objects: By tying smooth objects of uniform size such as marbles into small rosettes, you can dye a series of identical shapes. (The marbles make perfect circles.)

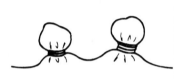

KNOTS AND FOLDS

Basic techniques

Fold dyeing: The knots described on the opposite page and block dyeing, at right, can be combined with folding which lets you repeat a specific motif. By folding the fabric horizontally, vertically, or diagonally, you can set up rhythms, with each repeat a mirror image of the pattern next to it. Folds are also used to change the direction of stripes in making squares, chevrons, and other linear designs.

Used by itself, without tying or blocking, fold dyeing is of limited usefulness on fabric. But it can produce beautiful designs on rice paper and other porous surfaces. To try this, fold paper towels into fan or flag shapes; then dip each edge of the paper into a different color of food coloring or concentrated dye solution. Other colors can be inserted between the fold lines with an eyedropper. Designs such as the one made of tissue paper on page 2488 merit framing. Clothespins and paper clips are useful for securing complicated folds during dyeing.

Block dyeing: You can dye a hard-edged design with two identical wood blocks and a C-clamp. Sandwich the folded fabric between the blocks and tighten the clamp. Since the dye cannot penetrate under the blocks, in effect you have created a negative stencil in a repeat pattern. The folded fabric should not be thick or the clamps may slip and the dye will not penetrate to the edge of the blocks. Take special care to make sure that even pressure is exerted by the blocks on the fabric so dye does not seep under the edges of the blocks.

Sew dyeing: Sewing the tie-dyeing knots into fabric takes more time than wrapping them with elastic bands, but it enables you to create more intricate designs. Anything you can do with an elastic band—and more—you can do with a needle and thread. Rather than pleating along a line to make a stripe, for example, sew running stitches along it, pull the end of the thread to gather the fabric, wrap the thread tightly around the fold line, and tie securely before dyeing. Fold designs can be sewn by first drawing a symmetrical pattern, such as a butterfly wing, a heart, a leaf, or a pear, along a folded edge. With running stitches, follow this line and pull the free end of the thread to gather the fabric. Wind the thread around the gathered fabric and tie it before dyeing.

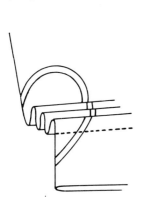

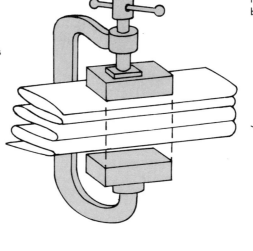

To develop your tie-dyeing skills, make puppets like these. The pattern is given on the grid at right. To enlarge the pattern, draw a grid of ½-inch squares; then copy the pattern lines, one square at a time.

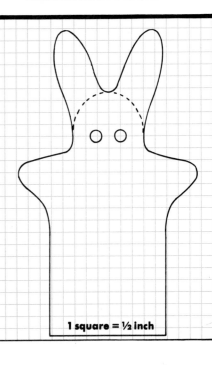

1 square = ½ inch

Paint and Color
Knotted and folded T-shirts ¢ ⌛ 👫 🏺

Using only the stripe knot and the bunch knot (Craftnotes, page 2474) you can make all of the T-shirt designs shown below. Stripe knots make controlled, symmetrical designs, such as outlines of hearts or butterflies, while bunch knots, tied at random, create soft, free-form impressions. The following instructions are for the blue-banded T-shirt, worn by the man at right. You can use the same knots, following Figures A, B, and C on page 2479 to make the other T-shirts shown.

Only two of the basic knots described in the Craftnotes (page 2474)—stripe and bunch—were used as ties to make all of these T-shirt designs. But each design is very different from the others.

In addition to the basic tie-dye materials listed on page 2470, you will need: a white cotton T-shirt or leotard; a pencil; a ruler; two empty squeeze-bottle applicators; and three colors of dye. (We used undiluted blue and yellow liquid dyes and a package of wine-colored powdered dye to make the blue-banded shirt.)

Knotting and Dyeing

To begin, wet the fabric with cold water. To remove excess moisture, run the shirt through the spin cycle of a washing machine or wring it well. Then lay the shirt, front up, on the work surface. With a pencil and ruler, draw guidelines for the blue band on the front of the shirt (photograph 1, page 2478). Fill the squeeze-bottle applicators with the blue and yellow dye. Squeeze blue dye within the guidelines for the center band. Wearing rubber gloves, rub the dye into the fabric (photograph 2). Blot up excess dye with a sponge; then gather the dye area horizontally into ½-inch-wide pleats. Wind an elastic band tightly at the top and bottom edges of the dyed area to hold the pleats (photograph 3).

Don't worry if some of the blue dye has spread outside of the banded area. It will either become part of the design at the top of the shirt or will be covered with the wine dye at the bottom. Wrap a few extra bands at random over the blue pleats to keep them from absorbing other colors. Next, drip splashes of yellow and blue dye on the top of the shirt (photograph 4). (These will soak through to dye the back of the shirt, but you can add more dye on the back to ensure even coloring.) It is important to leave about half the shirt white since the colors will appear brighter if some white remains. After you have sprinkled on the blue and yellow dyes, wad the upper part of the shirt into a bunch knot (Craftnotes, page 2474), and wind it tightly with at least five elastic bands (photograph 5). Rinse the entire shirt in cold water to remove the excess dye squeezed out by the elastic bands.

Make a dyebath for coloring the lower part of the shirt. Dissolve half a package of wine-colored powdered dye in a one-gallon enamel pot that is three-quarters filled with hot water. (Half a package gives good results when you dye one or two shirts a dark shade. If you want a lighter shade, use less dye.) Using a large spoon, stir the dye until it dissolves; then submerge the entire shirt in the hot dyebath (photograph 6). The knotting will keep the wine dye from coloring the top part of the shirt, but the heat will set the earlier dyes and make them washfast. Set the pot over a low flame to simmer for one hour, stirring often to ensure even color. If you want to achieve the uneven color tones typical of tie dyeing, crowd the fabric into a smaller pot. Then pour just enough concentrated liquid dye and water over the fabric to cover it. Do not stir the fabric as it simmers in this dyebath. After an hour of simmering, put on rubber gloves and remove the shirt from the dyebath; then rinse it in cold running water until the water runs clear.

Untie the knotted areas one at a time, working from dark to light. First remove the blue-stripe bands and rinse the blue area until the water runs clear. Then remove the bunch bands and rinse the shirt again until the water runs clear. (You can use a jet-spray sprinkler in a sink or a garden hose outdoors to speed rinsing.) Lay the shirt flat on an old towel to dry, or spin dry in a washing machine. To determine if the dyes are really colorfast, do not add the shirt to your normal load when you wash it for the first time.

Interlocking Ideas

To dye the other T-shirts pictured opposite, follow the general procedures above and the special instructions given with Figures A, B, and C (page 2479). You will be able to make borders, squares, flowers, stars, and complicated abstract designs as you gain experience in pleating and tying the fabric. Remember that colors applied with squeeze bottles can smear and make blotches in any solid-color area. To minimize this, be very neat while you drip dye and tie knots. Frequently wipe the work surface with a sponge to keep dye from being picked up by the fabric where you don't want it. For the ground color (wine in the case of the example above), choose a color dark enough to conceal blotches. If you plan to dye the fabric a light color, such as yellow, and there is a dark blotch on it, such as blue, you must remove the blue before you dye the fabric. But if the blotch is light, simply wash the tied bundle in warm water and detergent, or put ½ teaspoon of liquid dishwashing detergent into the dyebath; then dye as usual.

1: To tie dye the blue-banded T-shirt, start by drawing parallel pencil lines across the front of the shirt using a pencil and ruler. The top line connects the arm seams; the second line is 3 inches lower.

2: Squeeze blue liquid dye between the pencil lines. Then, wearing rubber gloves, use your forefinger to press the dye through both layers of fabric. Roll the dye toward the guidelines to get an even band.

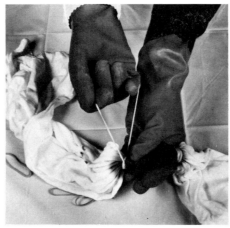

3: Fold the blue band evenly in ½-inch-wide pleats; then bind it at each end with an elastic band. Fasten at least five more bands between the first two to secure the folds so additional dye will not penetrate.

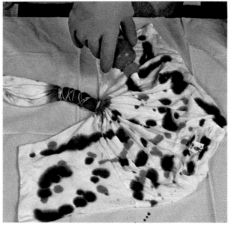

4: Sprinkle yellow and blue liquid dye above the blue folds, covering the neck, shoulders, and sleeves. Leave about half of the shirt area white, between drips, to keep the design crisp. Make sure the dye penetrates both layers.

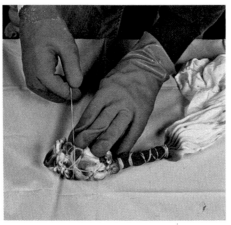

5: Crumple the top of the shirt into a bunch knot, as shown in the Craftnotes on page 2474. Secure these folds by randomly wrapping them with elastic bands. Rinse the shirt in cold water to remove excess dye squeezed out from under the banding.

6: When all of the knots are in place, dissolve powdered dye in a three-gallon pot three-quarters full of hot water. Submerge the entire shirt in the dyebath and set the pot over low heat for one hour, stirring frequently.

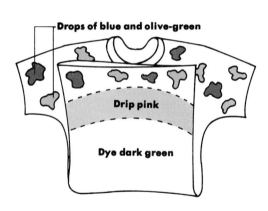

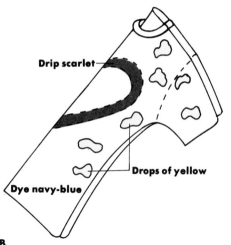

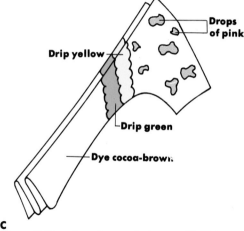

A

Figure A: To make a repeated-arc design as shown on the pink and green T-shirt on page 2476, fold the bottom of the shirt up as shown, aligning it with the inner edge of the neck band. With a pencil, mark a point 2 inches from the bottom edge of the shirt. Connect this point with both under-arms to form an arc. Three inches below this line, draw an identical arc. Spread pink dye within the arc and gather this area in ¾-inch-wide folds. Secure the folds by wrapping the dyed area with elastic bands. Drip even amounts of blue and olive-green dye above the top edge of the tied area and gather that portion into a bunch knot. Let the tied shirt simmer in a dark-green dyebath.

B

Figure B: To dye a heart on a T-shirt, as shown on page 2476, fold the shirt in half lengthwise. Place guide dots on the fold 5 inches below the neck band and 10 inches above the bottom edge. Put another dot 1 inch in from the underarm, and connect these points to form half a heart shape. Pencil a second heart 2 inches inside the first. Spread scarlet dye within the heart border. Gather the dyed area into folds on a diagonal, following the curve of the heart, and band securely. Splash yellow dye liberally outside the folded area, and tie the shirt with bunch knots above and below the banded area. Simmer the shirt in a navy-blue dyebath for one hour, stirring frequently.

C

Figure C: To make a chevron design on a T-shirt like the one on page 2476, fold a shirt in half lengthwise; then fold each side seam back to meet the center fold. With a pencil and ruler, mark guide dots along the folded edge 6, 8, and 10 inches below the neck band and 1, 3, and 5 inches below the underarm seam. Connect each pair of dots with a straight line to form two diagonal stripes. Fill in the upper stripe with yellow dye and the lower one with green dye. Pleat the stripes on a diagonal and tie with elastic bands. Tie the stripes carefully, or you may get a scalloped design. Drip pink dye along the sleeves, and tie in a bunch knot. Simmer the shirt in a brown dyebath.

Paint and Color
Tie-dye stitchery ¢ ⌛ 🚶 🦃

The scarf and skirt shown on page 2481 each began as a rectangle of white silk. Sewn with butterfly-shaped knots (Craftnotes, page 2475), the wet piece of folded fabric was dipped into a light-colored dyebath. Sewing was repeated several times between different colors of dye until the color combination pictured was achieved.

Although for the scarf we used the sew-dyeing technique on a 22-by-52-inch piece of white silk surah, you can substitute any thin fabric, such as cotton, chiffon, batiste, organdy, or gingham. In addition to the tie-dyeing materials listed on page 2470, you will need: a pencil; 4-by-7-inch sheets of tracing paper and cardboard; scissors; white glue; a needle and strong linen thread; and a pot large enough to hold the fabric comfortably. We used a three-gallon pot, and powdered turquoise, fuchsia, and yellow dye. You can use any color combination you like, of course.

Trace the butterfly-wing pattern (Figure D, page 2480). Cut out this tracing and trace it on the cardboard. Cut out the cardboard pattern. Rinse the fabric in cold water and wring well. Put the fabric right-side up on the work surface and fold it diagonally, vertically, or horizontally. With a pencil, trace the butterfly-wing pattern several times along the fold (photograph 7, page 2480). Stitch the pattern outline through both layers of fabric, using running stitches spaced every 1/4 inch (photograph 8). Gather the fabric each time you pass a curve. Compress the gathers neatly with thread and tie. Wrap one or two elastic bands around the gathers between the knotted thread and the folded edge (photograph 9).

Trace, sew, knot, and band the design wherever you want a white butterfly. (If the fabric starts to get dry, sprinkle it with cold water before you dye it.) Next, dissolve half a package of turquoise dye in the pot, half-filled with hot water. Submerge the entire piece of fabric in this dyebath and simmer over a low flame for about 15 minutes. Stir frequently to promote even dyeing. Follow the directions on the package of dye, and to ensure even dyeing, make sure the pot is large enough to accommodate the fabric easily. If the results are uneven, add a little dishwashing

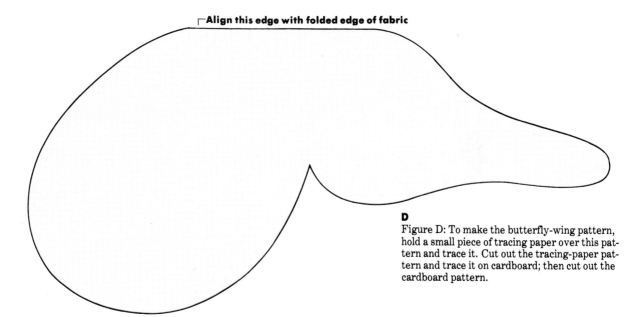

Align this edge with folded edge of fabric

D

Figure D: To make the butterfly-wing pattern, hold a small piece of tracing paper over this pattern and trace it. Cut out the tracing-paper pattern and trace it on cardboard; then cut out the cardboard pattern.

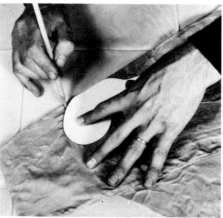

7: To start sew-dyeing the butterfly scarf, align the straight edge of the butterfly pattern with a folded edge of fabric. Trace the pattern outline on the cloth with a pencil. Patterns should be spaced evenly for a repeat design.

8: Starting at one end of the pattern along the fold, sew the pattern outline through both layers of fabric with ¼-inch running stitches. To gather the wet fabric, bunch the stitched areas frequently.

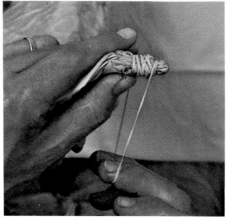

9: Gather the stitched fabric tightly and end the thread with a double knot. Wind elastic bands above the knot to compress the folds and prevent the knotted area from absorbing dye. A fringed edge will be left around the butterfly wings.

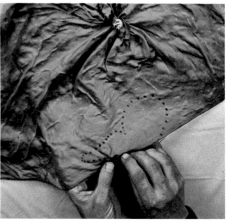

10: To follow the pattern as you stitch and gather the butterflies, evenly space guide dots on its outline with a waterproof marker. With sewing complete, place the cloth in the fuchsia dyebath. Then rinse the fabric well before removing the knots.

detergent to the dyebath. Rinse the dyed fabric in cold water, being careful not to loosen the knotted and bound areas. Squeeze the fabric lightly to remove excess moisture before stitching additional designs.

Double Dipped

To make the turquoise butterflies, follow the same procedure you used to make white ones (photograph 10). Prepare a fuchsia dyebath and again dye the fabric for 15 minutes, stirring frequently. By covering the turquoise areas with fuchsia, you will get a rich purple, while the knotted areas will remain white and turquoise. Rinse the fabric well.

Finally, sew, knot, and band more butterflies in the purple silk. Put one package of yellow dye and 1 teaspoon of detergent in a pot three-quarters filled with hot water. Simmer the fabric for at least half an hour in the yellow bath. This will turn the purple to a warm brown tone. Rinse the fabric until the water runs clear. Then carefully remove the knots, rinsing one color at a time, working from dark to light to reveal the purple, turquoise, and white butterfly designs. Iron the fabric while it is still damp.

Using the technique of sewing designs into fabric rather than holding them with elastic bands, silk was dyed with a butterfly design to make a skirt and matching scarf.

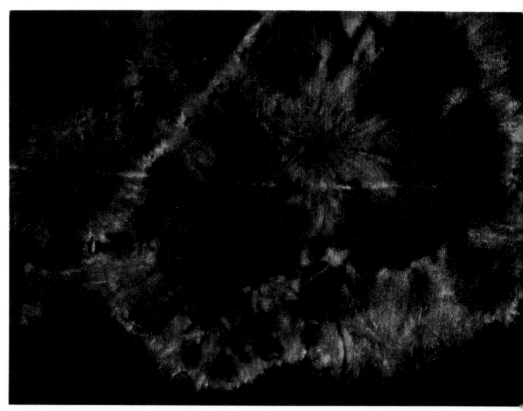

This closeup detail of the table throw pictured opposite shows the patterns of radiant light blue and green that were revealed when doughnut knots were untied. Elastic bands leave light-colored areas and soft edges about the designs that set them off from the dark-colored, evenly dyed border.

Paint and Color
Velvet table throw

To make the table throw shown above and on the opposite page, closely spaced doughnut knots (Craftnotes, page 2474) were tied in the center of a piece of turquoise rayon velvet. Then green, yellow, and blue dyes were poured over the knots and the border was dunked in dark-green dye. This same piece of dyed fabric could be bound with open hems to make a wall hanging like the one shown on page 2487, or backed and stuffed to make a large floor cushion.

To make the table throw you need 2 yards of 36-inch-wide turquoise rayon velvet or any other thick, plush material. If you use rayon velvet, you will need: a bottle of muriatic acid (available at drugstores); metal tongs; and rubber gloves. In addition to the tie-dye materials listed on page 2470, you need: a ruler; a water-base felt-tipped marker; elastic bands; a three-gallon pot; three empty plastic applicator bottles; and white glue. We used kelly green, yellow, and blue liquid dyes and a dark-green powdered dye to complement the turquoise color of the fabric chosen. (The amount of dye needed will vary with the size of the fabric.)

To prepare the fabric so the dye will be absorbed while the vibrant color is retained, remove the permanent-press treatment by simmering the velvet in a solution of ½ teaspoon of muriatic acid to 2 gallons of water for 30 minutes. Use metal tongs to remove the fabric from the solution. Wearing rubber gloves, rinse the fabric in cold water and wring well. (If you do not want to remove the permanent-press finish with acid, wash the velvet thoroughly but do not rinse out all of the detergent; the soapy film will help the fabric absorb dye.)

To begin, fold the wet velvet in half lengthwise and lay it flat on the work surface. With a ruler and a water-base marking pen, make a line of dots 10 inches from each raw edge (photograph 11, page 2484). This forms a rectangle in the center of the fabric adjacent to the fold. Through the double thickness of the folded fabric, make

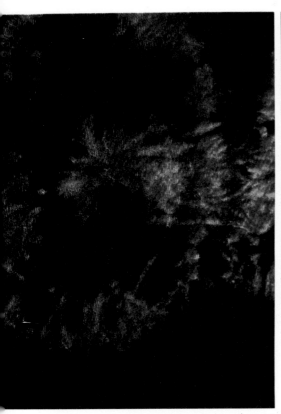

The rayon-velvet table throw (right) was tied with doughnut knots (Craftnotes, page 2474). Then the knots were sprinkled with blue, yellow, and green dye. The border was simmered in a bath of dark-green dye, with the knots floating on the surface.

doughnut knots (Craftnotes, page 2474) at each corner of the rectangle. In the same way, make a series of doughnut knots just inside the dotted lines of the rectangle (photograph 12, page 2484). The guidelines of the rectangle should be visible just below the bands so you can tell that they are in a straight line. If space doesn't permit a full doughnut knot, tie a rosette knot (Craftnotes, page 2474), distorting its shape if necessary to follow the line.

Next, fill the area inside the rectangle with doughnut knots. For best results, keep them as close together as possible. With all of the knots fastened in place, fill the applicator bottles with yellow, blue, and green liquid dye. First squirt yellow dye into the center of each doughnut knot. Then pour a ring of blue above the banded base of each knot. Trickle kelly green dye liberally between the knots; then sprinkle a few drops on top of each knot (photograph 13).

To dye the border a solid color, dissolve a 1⅛-ounce package of dark-green powdered dye in a three-gallon pot, filled three-quarters full with hot water. Lower the raw edges of the velvet into the pot. Submerge the border completely in the dyebath, leaving the doughnut knots floating on the surface. Knots tend to sink when they are left unattended, but you can rest them against the rim of the pot between stirrings. Leave the border in the simmering dyebath for one hour. Stir the dyebath every ten minutes by holding the knots and dunking the border gently in the dye (photograph 14). This allows air bubbles trapped between the knots and the dye surface to escape.

With the colors used, it did not matter that the dark-green color of the dyebath splashed onto the knots. But for maximum color contrast between the knotted design and the border, keep the knots elevated above the surface of the dyebath.

When the dyeing is completed, rinse the fabric in cold running water until the water runs clear. Then untie the knots and rinse again. To remove excess moisture, run the velvet through the spin cycle of a washing machine; then hang it on a line to dry. Fold the raw edges under about 1 inch on all sides and fasten the hem with white glue, or finish the edges with evenly spaced running stitches every ½ inch.

11: To mark a rectangle in the center of the table throw, fold the velvet in half lengthwise and use a water-base black marker and ruler to put rows of guide dots 10 inches in from the unfolded edges. Evenly space the guide dots every one inch.

12: Tie doughnut knots (Craftnotes, page 2474), incorporating both layers of fabric, along each dotted line. Make the knots close together so the soft edges of the design will not be obscured by the border color.

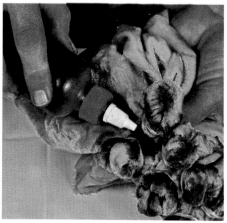

13: To color the table-throw design, squirt yellow dye in the opening of each knot. Then pour a ring of blue dye above the bands of each knot. Liberally apply kelly-green dye between the bases of the knots. Any unwanted dye that spreads on the border will be covered in the dark color of the dyebath.

14: Submerge the untied areas in the dark-green dyebath, leaving the knots floating on the surface. To promote even dyeing, agitate the border by holding the top of two knots at opposite ends of the cloth, thus letting trapped air bubbles escape. In this way, fabric above the base of each knot will absorb the dark color of the dyebath.

Paint and Color
Block-dyeing a design $

Block dyeing and fold dyeing (both described in the Craftnotes, page 2475) were combined to create the wall hanging shown on page 2487.

For the hanging, you need a 42-by-64-inch piece of cotton batiste. (Remember that dye colors are brightest if there is no permanent-press finish.) In addition to materials listed on page 2470, you need: a pencil; a ruler; two 1-by-2-by-8-inch wood blocks; two 4-inch C-clamps; tightly woven cord; a three-gallon pot; two empty squeeze-bottle applicators; yellow and scarlet liquid dye; and a package of cocoa-brown powdered dye.

Folding the Fabric

Wash the cotton batiste and remove excess water by running it through the spin cycle of a washing machine. Then fold the damp cotton in half lengthwise. Locate the midpoint of the folded edge and fold as shown in Figure E, opposite. Next, fold

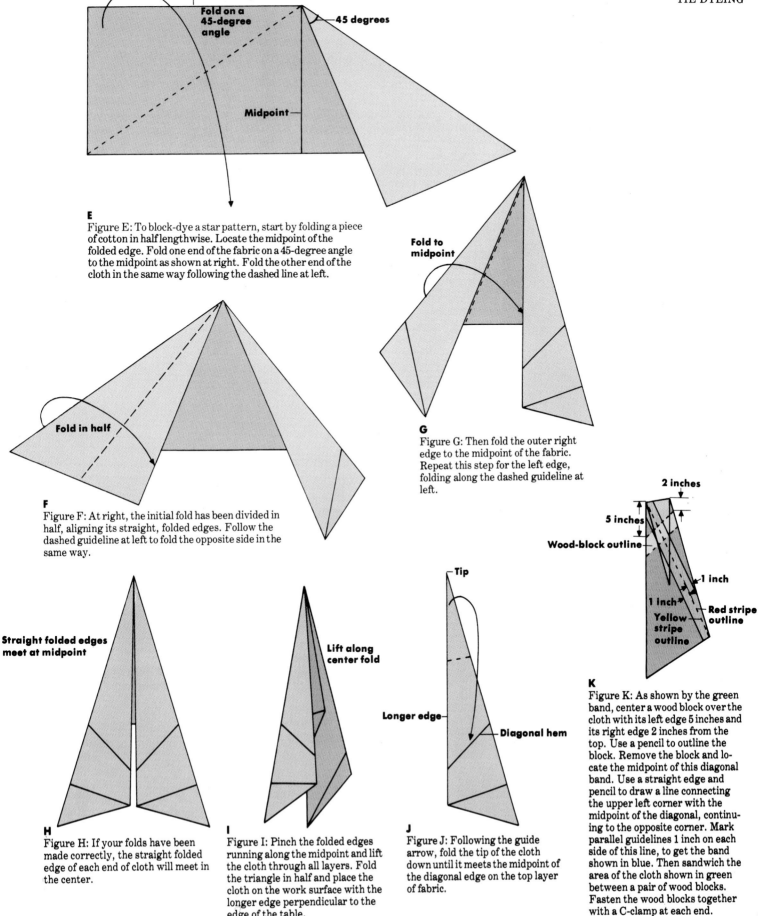

Folded edge

Fold on a 45-degree angle

45 degrees

Midpoint

E

Figure E: To block-dye a star pattern, start by folding a piece of cotton in half lengthwise. Locate the midpoint of the folded edge. Fold one end of the fabric on a 45-degree angle to the midpoint as shown at right. Fold the other end of the cloth in the same way following the dashed line at left.

Fold to midpoint

G

Figure G: Then fold the outer right edge to the midpoint of the fabric. Repeat this step for the left edge, folding along the dashed guideline at left.

Fold in half

F

Figure F: At right, the initial fold has been divided in half, aligning its straight, folded edges. Follow the dashed guideline at left to fold the opposite side in the same way.

Straight folded edges meet at midpoint

Lift along center fold

Tip

2 inches

5 inches

Wood-block outline

1 inch

1 inch

Yellow stripe outline

Red stripe outline

Longer edge

Diagonal hem

H

Figure H: If your folds have been made correctly, the straight folded edge of each end of cloth will meet in the center.

I

Figure I: Pinch the folded edges running along the midpoint and lift the cloth through all layers. Fold the triangle in half and place the cloth on the work surface with the longer edge perpendicular to the edge of the table.

J

Figure J: Following the guide arrow, fold the tip of the cloth down until it meets the midpoint of the diagonal edge on the top layer of fabric.

K

Figure K: As shown by the green band, center a wood block over the cloth with its left edge 5 inches and its right edge 2 inches from the top. Use a pencil to outline the block. Remove the block and locate the midpoint of this diagonal band. Use a straight edge and pencil to draw a line connecting the upper left corner with the midpoint of the diagonal, continuing to the opposite corner. Mark parallel guidelines 1 inch on each side of this line, to get the band shown in blue. Then sandwich the area of the cloth shown in green between a pair of wood blocks. Fasten the wood blocks together with a C-clamp at each end.

outer triangles in half as shown in Figure F, page 2485. Fold the triangles once more so they meet in a straight line along the midpoint (Figure G). The result is shown in Figure H. With your hands, hold the top and bottom of the folded edges along the midpoint. Then pinch and lift all layers and fold the cloth in half again vertically (Figure I).

Next, fold the point of the cloth inward to center it along the top diagonal edge that runs across the cloth (Figure J). Minor mistakes in folding may change the design; so make sure that you have followed these directions carefully.

Fixing Pattern Guidelines and Wood Blocks

Before drawing the designs on the cloth, soak the pair of wood blocks and eight 12-inch lengths of cotton string in warm water. When fastened around the cloth, the string and blocks will keep the fabric from absorbing dye. Place a wood block over the folded cloth, positioning it on a diagonal as shown in green in Figure K. With a pencil, trace the top and bottom edges of the block on the cloth; then remove the block. With ruler and pencil, mark parallel lines along the length of the fabric (enclosing the blue band in Figure K). To do this, draw a straight line from the upper left-hand corner of the folded edge, through the midpoint of the wood-block guidelines, and intersect the corner of the fabric diagonally opposite. Draw straight lines 1 inch on either side of this line. Then put the wood block back in place, and back it with the second block under the fabric. Tighten a C-clamp ½ inch from each end of the wood blocks, making sure the fabric and blocks do not slip. The metal clamps should not touch the fabric.

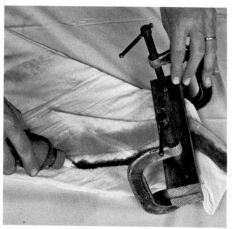

15: With wood blocks clamped in place, first squirt yellow dye within the marked guidelines. Rub the dye through all layers of the cloth, working it toward the guidelines. (It is advisable to wear rubber gloves when you touch the dye.) Then apply red dye to make an adjacent stripe in the same way.

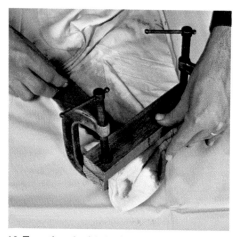

16: To gather the fabric, fold the dyed area above the wood blocks neatly in ¾-inch folds working toward the top edge of the wood blocks. Holding these pleats in place, fold the dyed area remaining below the bottom edge of the wood blocks in the same way.

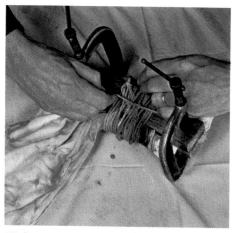

17: Center a wet string between the red and yellow stripe, and tie the string about the cloth and blocks. Wrap the yellow and then the red areas with wet string. Place the blocked cloth in a brown dyebath and simmer over low heat for one hour. Push and pull the clamps protruding from the dyebath to rotate the cloth and promote even dyeing.

Dyeing and Pleating the Star Design

Fill two squeeze bottles with yellow and red liquid dye. Dribble a 1-inch-wide band of yellow dye to make a stripe with the band marked with pencil. Wearing rubber gloves, gently press the dye into the cloth so all layers will absorb it. Add more dye along the reverse side of the fabric sandwich if the dye has not penetrated evenly. To the right of the yellow stripe, drip a 1-inch-wide band of red dye (photograph 15). Work the red dye into the cloth in the same way. Since the cloth was first saturated with yellow dye, the fabric is wet enough to keep the band of red dye from bleeding onto the yellow area. Next, gather the dyed areas neatly in ¾-inch folds, working from the edges of the fabric toward the blocks. Hold the first folds above the top edge of the blocks as you carefully fold the lower area toward the bottom edge (photograph 16). Press the folds against the edges of the blocks, and tie a wet string around the fabric to separate the yellow and red stripes. Then tie another string around each end of the pleated fabric to hold the folds in place as you continue tying the fabric around the wood blocks. Tie more wet string around the yellow area until it is completely bound with string. Repeat in the same way until the red area is covered (photograph 17).

Final Dyebath

With the 2-inch-wide dyed area fastened securely, prepare the final dyebath. To do this, dissolve one-half package of brown powdered dye in a three-gallon pot that is filled with enough hot water to cover the blocks and fabric. Set the pot over a low flame to simmer for about one hour. To ensure even dyeing, rotate the fabric by holding the handles of the clamps that extend above the surface of the dyebath and swinging them gently back and forth. To remove the fabric from the dye, lift by the clamps. Run the blocked and tied fabric under cold water until the water runs clear of brown dye. As the red dye is more difficult to rinse out than yellow dye, untie the red section first and rinse it thoroughly before you untie the yellow area. When the water runs completely clear of yellow dye, remove the clamps and unfold the fabric. Spin in a washing machine; then iron the fabric while it is still slightly damp.

If you want to display the fabric as a wall hanging, make 1½-inch hems on the top and bottom. Insert 52-inch curtain rods or dowels in the hems and rest the ends of the top rod on brackets or nails.

For related entries see "Batik," "Block Printing," "Linoleum and Woodcuts," "Monoprinting," "Neckties," and "Vegetable Dyes."

This cotton-batiste wall hanging was made with wood blocks, the intricate folding diagramed on page 2485, and three dyebaths. An open hem along the top edge permits hanging on a curtain rod.

Paper can be folded and dyed to make designs suitable for framing. This rectangular piece of tissue paper was folded until the entire piece formed a triangle, resembling a folded flag. One tip of the triangle along the hypotenuse was dipped in red dye and the other end in blue. When the paper dried, it was opened to reveal this soft-edged circle and diamond pattern.

In the city of Jaipur, India, craftsmen dye tiny rectangular patterns like these by tying grains of rice into silk with thread. First the silk is wet thoroughly; then it is stretched over a board drilled with tiny holes. As the fabric dries, it conforms to the surface. The dyers use the sunken areas as guide dots for inserting rice. The cloth is gathered about each grain of rice. The rice is held in place with a continuous strand of fine thread.

The fabric of this caftan, a piece of white chiffon that was folded and tie dyed between matching wood blocks, is as precisely patterned as any printed fabric. The wood blocks were skillfully cut to resemble feathers—an advanced application of the technique described in page 2484. Windup knots were tied about the chest and shoulders to create sunburst patterns. The Richardsons tie-dyed this creation by combining the basic techniques described on the previous pages.

Rochelle Lapidus is a professional graphic designer, a painter, and a lapidary. She has long been intrigued by the challenge of transforming abstract ideas into visual realities. "The concept of time is one of the most difficult to capture," she says, "because it never stands still."

Time is one of the more baffling aspects of our world—and one of the more elusive. Men have long tried to get to the heart of it, to understand how they are situated in it, where it is coming from, where it is leading. But all that is really known about it is how to mark its relentless movement. The projects that follow do just this.

These clever (and once common) devices for telling time are simple to make and use. They are especially appealing if you are willing to sacrifice split-second accuracy. Your ancestors did not attempt to measure precisely the packages that time comes in, but they measured time with ample accuracy for their needs. They could more or less tell where they were in the day simply by observing the progression of shadows. When greater precision was needed, they could consult a sundial. In cloudy weather they could tell time by measuring the length of a burning candle or rope, or the amount of water or sand that accumulated below a constantly dripping source. On a clear night, they could tell time by the position of the stars.

Today, such devices and methods are not accurate enough for many purposes. But their appeal lives on. The projects here, in an antiquarian spirit, include a noon mark for checking your watch by the sun, a candle clock for measuring time, an egg-timer sandglass, and a nocturnal dial that will add a new dimension to star-gazing.

How Time Has Changed

No one has any trouble discerning what a day is, but its divisions—the hours, minutes, and seconds of time telling—are artificial and arbitrary inventions. There were not always 24 hours in a day, and hours were not always 60 minutes long. The first people to divide a day into 12 parts—perhaps the Babylonians of 2000 B. C.— did not at first set periods of fixed duration, but rather cut equal fractions from the total daylight on any given day. Thus, the length of an hour varied depending on the duration of daylight at different times of the year. Nights, as late as post-Roman times, did not consist of 12 hours but of four quarters called vigils. In winter, vigils expanded to fill the long nights. The opposite was true in summer. It was only a few centuries ago that a day was divided into 24 equal parts.

Ancient and modern time telling have one thing in common—the way noon can be determined by the sun. Noon is the center of the day—halfway between sunrise and sunset—and it is the best point for reckoning other times. Noon is also the easiest time to determine. By definition, it is the moment when the sun is highest in the sky and, in the northern hemisphere, directly south of the observer.

Designs and Decorations
A light show at noon

¢ ▨ 👫 🎨

The fact that the sun is directly south at noon has been used in the construction of a variety of midday indicators. One sultan of Morocco had a cannon that fired automatically at noon, sparked by a carefully positioned magnifying glass when the sun's rays reached the right angle. In similar fashion, an electric range controlled by a photoelectric cell can heat water in a tea kettle and produce a noon whistle. Other noon indicators were common before clocks and watches became widely available. In many places, people would gather just before noon in a public place where there was a noon mark. The most common mark consisted merely of a north-south line on the ground or a building facade, with a pole so positioned that its shadow fell along the line at the moment of noon. To make a noon mark, all you need to know is how to determine true north or south (not the magnetic north indicated by a compass). One way is to draw a line pointing to the North Star (Figure A).

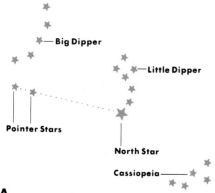

A
Figure A: To draw a true north-south line, needed for some nonmechanical clocks, find the North Star; then draw a line that points to it. The northern constellations revolve around the virtually motionless North Star like hands on a clock. To locate the North Star, extend an imaginary line from the Pointer Stars of the Big Dipper (the two outer stars of its cup).

The sands of time filter through the narrow neck of a classic figure-eight egg timer. Making such simple instruments to tell time is almost a lost art. The projects that follow include an egg timer that works like this one but is made without blown glass.

Just before noon, a shaft of sunlight approaches the noon mark, a reflective strip of foil. The line of light moves from west to east as the sun moves from east to west.

A noon mark fleetingly catches the sun at the midpoint of the day. A noon mark can be any device that casts a shaft of light or a shadow on a north-south line at the moment of noon. This one consists of a long, thin opening cut in a piece of cardboard and a strip of reflective foil. The cardboard with its vertical cutout is in a window that faces south. At noon, sun time, a shaft of sunlight falls on the foil, making it glow.

Correcting for Local Time

When you use a noon mark, you will probably find that it does not agree with your watch, due to modern timekeeping conventions. The most obvious is daylight saving time. When it is in effect, a noon mark becomes a 1 P.M. mark.

Another factor is standard time, which standardizes time within zones that are 15 longitudinal degrees wide. True noon, however, arrives 4 minutes later for each longitudinal degree, east to west. To make an adjustment for standard time, consult a map or almanac to determine your longitude to within 1 degree of accuracy. Compare it to the standard meridian for the time zone where you live. In the United States, this is 75 degrees for the eastern zone, 90 for central, 105 for mountain, and 120 for pacific. If the two are the same, no adjustment is necessary. If they differ and you are east of the standard meridian (your longitude is a lower number), the noon mark will be faster than standard time by 4 minutes for each degree of longitude. And if you live west of the standard meridian, the noon mark will be correspondingly slower.

A third factor that may cause a watch to differ from a noon mark is the sun's cyclical fluctuation. The sun loses and gains speed at certain times of the year by a few seconds each day. In a year, this difference accumulates to as much as 16 minutes before the cycle reverses itself and balance is restored.

To adjust for this fluctuation, refer to Figure B. It tells the number of minutes your watch will be faster or slower than a noon shadow on any day of the year.

To make the noon mark agree with your watch, subtract an hour from watch time when daylight saving time is in effect, add or subtract 4 minutes for each degree of difference from the standard meridian, and add or subtract the number of minutes shown in Figure B for that day's date.

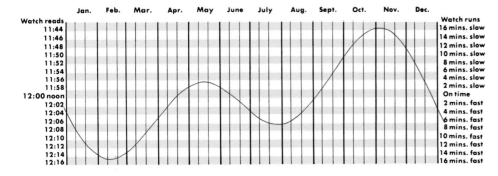

B

Figure B: Fluctuations in the sunlight cycle create a difference of up to 16 minutes between an accurate noon mark and an accurate clock, depending on the time of year. To find out how much slower or faster than the sun your timepiece will be at any season, estimate the date on the horizontal scale at the top of this graph. Extend an imaginary vertical line from this point down to the red line on the graph. From the point where the two lines meet, imagine a third line moving horizontally to the right, and there read the number of minutes your watch will be fast or slow when the noon mark indicates midday.

A Noon Beam Reflector

To make a noon mark more interesting, you can arrange it to trigger a modest light show, as pictured opposite, at the moment of noon. Instead of using a shadow-casting pole, let a shaft of light fall on a reflective noon line. Cut a piece of cardboard or opaque paper the size of one of the panes in a south-facing window. In the center of the cardboard, cut a vertical opening ½ inch wide and 12 or more inches long. Put the cardboard over one of the window's lower panes. Devise a horizontal surface (perhaps a tabletop) that extends from the windowsill, so the beam of light that passes through the slit will be clearly visible. Cut a strip of aluminum foil 2 inches wide and 2 feet or more long. Place the strip on the horizontal surface to make a true north-south line, starting directly below the vertical opening.

During the morning, the beam will move toward the reflective strip—the photograph at far left was taken at 11:45 A.M. A few minutes before noon, the beam will reach the edge of the reflective strip, causing it to begin to gleam. The reflection will be most intense as the beam reaches the center of the strip at the precise moment of noon, then will gradually diminish until it passes off the reflective strip.

Designs and Decorations
A candle clock

An old method of marking the passing hours was to burn a calibrated candle. In the days when people made their own candles, they could control the dimensions and ingredients to achieve candles that burned at a reasonably constant and predictable rate. They could determine—with a few careful experiments—how fast a candle would burn, then cut notches or insert markers to tell time. A candle cannot, of course, be used to tell time directly, but it can be used to measure the time elapsed since it was lighted. So if the starting time is known—as, for example, by the noon-marker method described on page 2490—the candle does indeed tell time.

To make a candle clock like the one pictured below (left), buy a small supply of long, thin, tapered factory-made candles. Untapered candles, especially those that are thick, are less suitable. If you get all the candles from one source, they will burn almost identically. Put one candle in a candle holder, and place the holder on an old plate to catch the drippings. With a ruler or yardstick, measure the candle from the base of the wick to the top of the holder. Record this dimension, light the candle in a draft-free place, and record the time when you lit it. As the candle burns, measure the height to the base of the wick at set intervals—say every 5, 10, or 15 minutes. Be careful not to burn yourself, and do not leave a burning candle unattended. Record the measurement and time for each reading.

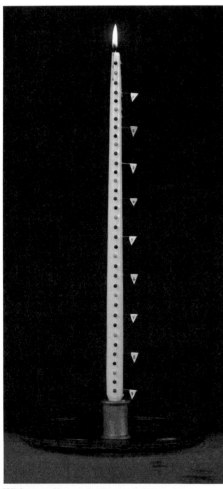

With an ordinary wax taper and pins, you can make this unusual candle clock, perhaps as a party decoration for New Year's Eve. To make such a timer, calculate average burning time by experimenting; then insert pins at measured intervals into a second identical candle. As the hours burn away, the pins will drop to measure the passage of time. Paper flags, attached to the pins that mark the hours and numbered in sequence from top to bottom, are useful as well as decorative.

Candle clocks like this nineteenth-century model were used in many parts of the world both to illuminate and to keep track of the hours of darkness.

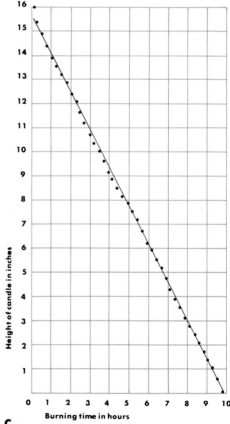

C

Figure C: This graph charts the melting rate of a candle identical to the one pictured in color at left. It provided the information needed to insert the time-telling pins in the candle. The graph's vertical scale represents the height of the candle, and its horizontal scale the duration of burning. The plotted points, which represent measurements taken at 15-minute intervals, form a nearly straight line. The rate of melting was about 1½ inches per hour.

When the candle is consumed, use a piece of graph paper to chart the measurements and times. Let the horizontal lines represent time and vertical lines the height of the candle. Plot these points as shown in Figure C. Using a ruler, connect the plotted points. You will probably find, as I did, that except for the first inch or so where the taper is extreme, the candle burned at a remarkably constant rate. This will be indicated by a nearly straight line of points on the graph.

If this is the case, divide the original height of the candle by the number of hours it burned to establish the average burning distance per hour. On identical candles, insert pins at intervals of this distance. (Allow a slightly larger interval between the base of the wick and the first pin.) From the moment you light one of the candles, each time the flame reaches a pin, an hour will have elapsed (give or take a few minutes). The pins will fall to the plate holding the candle as the flame reaches them, though they do not get hot. If you stick a paper flag onto each pin, numbered in sequence from top to bottom, you will have an every-hour alarm clock, assuming it is quiet enough to hear a pin drop.

If you want to mark more than just the hours, buy pushpins in four colors to mark the quarter hours. In the candle clock pictured in color, the hours are marked with red pins, the first quarters with green, the halves with yellow, and the third quarters with blue.

If the points on your graph paper do not approximate a straight line, this may be due to an extreme taper or to molten wax buildup at the base of the wick, which will affect the rate of burning. In this case, you can determine the location of each pin from the line on the graph paper. Insert the first pin at the height indicated for 1 hour of burning time, the second at the height for 2 hours, and so on. Marking time by measuring the rate at which something burned was commonly done in the past. A knotted length of smoldering fiber rope was widely used, despite its acrid smell. (Note: Some modern synthetic rope is dangerously flammable.) An indoor counterpart of the burning rope was the incense-stick clock of the ancient Chinese. It worked on the same principle but smelled better.

Glass and Plastics
A sandglass

The flow of water and sand has been widely used to keep time. The 500-year-old water clock shown at right was used in Canton, China, into the twentieth century. And the compound sandglass pictured on page 2496 was a precision instrument in its day—the eighteenth century. To this day, many kitchens and family rooms are equipped with miniature sandglasses to regulate three-minute eggs or five-minute turns in games.

You can improvise a sand or water clock using a large container, such as a bucket or heavy plastic bag, to serve as a reservoir for sand or water. First, make a hole in the reservoir—a pinhole for water, a larger hole (such as one made with a 6-penny nail) for sand. Place a large, clear, calibrated graduate below the reservoir to register the amount of sand or water that passes through the hole. Fill the reservoir and chart the accumulation per period of time, following the instructions for the candle clock (opposite). Flow clocks are more reliable than combustion clocks. A half-hour sample will let you calculate how many milliliters or ounces accumulate every five minutes. Flow clocks do pose one problem: the rate of flow is affected by pressure, so the contents of the reservoir must be replenished from time to time. Below a certain percentage of capacity, the rate of flow diminishes sharply. The Romans solved this problem by using huge reserve tanks that could drain all day without losing an appreciable percentage of the contents. The Chinese system shown at right uses a series of reservoirs to keep pressure constant in the key feeder, the second jar from the bottom.

One easy-to-make timer that uses sand flow is the egg-timer sandglass shown in color on page 2496. The traditional hourglass pictured on page 2491 cannot be made without great skill in glassblowing. But you can make a modern version with two plastic funnels, two glass or plastic containers, some sand (such as the colored sand sold in plant stores), and all-purpose transparent household cement. The funnels I

The water clock at Canton, China, more than five centuries old and still in use at the turn of the twentieth century, consisted of four copper jars, on a flight of steps, connected with small troughs. The largest jar held nearly 12 gallons. A wooden float, partly visible atop the lowest jar, marked the time as that jar filled with water. The attendant beat the 12 hours of the day on drums and at noon poured the water from the bottom jar back into the top one.

used were the 2-ounce plastic type sold in variety stores. I chose small glass apothecary jars for the containers, but any lightweight transparent cups, jars, or glasses will do, as long as they do not have indented necks that would keep the sand from falling freely, and have rims a smaller diameter than the funnel necks.

Assembling the Sandglass

With a single-edged razor blade or craft knife, cut the stem entirely off one of the funnels, and all but ¼ inch of stem off the other. Insert the stem into the hole as far as it will go. Cement the joint where the funnels meet, inside and out. Use enough cement around the projecting stem to fill the funnel to the top of the stem so sand will not be trapped in the joint. When the cement is dry, cement the rim of one of the containers to the inside of the funnel. When that cement is dry, pour about ½ cup of fine sand into this container through the double funnel, and measure the time it takes to run down into the container. This will probably be about three minutes. Add or remove sand until you reach the time period you want to measure. (One, three, five, and ten minutes are useful spans.) If you want a longer span than the capacity of the container allows, use cement to diminish the diameter of the funnel hole. Keep a toothpick handy to reopen the hole if it gets clogged with cement. Test the flow time several times, pouring the sand in and out of the container until you are sure you have the right amount. Then cement the rim of the second container inside the second funnel.

A four-part hourglass from the eighteenth century divides the hour into quarters. The four chambers, containing different amounts of sand, would empty at 15-minute intervals. Sometimes an attendant would have the task of announcing the time and inverting the apparatus when an hour had elapsed.

A three-minute egg timer in the traditional hourglass shape does not have to be made of blown glass. This one is made with two plastic funnels, two transparent containers, and some colored sand. The cost was less than a dollar.

Outdoor Activities
A star dial

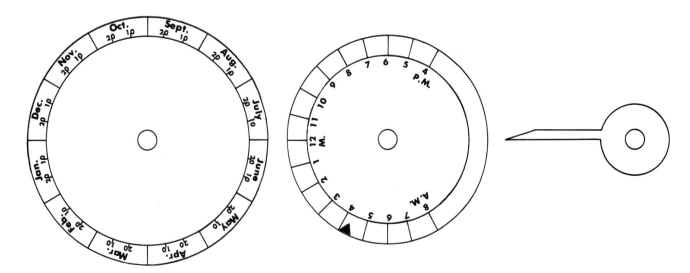

D
Figure D: To make a nocturnal, transfer these three full-sized shapes onto stiff cardboard and cut them out. Make a hole in the center of each shape so you can turn them onto a threaded rod.

Except for the noon mark (which has limited usefulness) the burning candles and running sand described on pages 2494 through 2496 measure only the passage of time. Strictly speaking, they do not tell what time it is at all. They must be set in motion at a known moment or they have no practical use. But the ancients made them work, even though they had no timepieces for regulating them. Two clever methods were widely used, the sundial, well known to this day, and its almost forgotten counterpart, the nocturnal, a device that looks something like a lollipop. The nocturnal pictured on page 2498 is simple enough for a child to make and use.

Because northern constellations rotate around the North Star (Figure A, page 2490) approximately once a day you can tell the time of night by observing their position. But in addition to the nightly movement, the stars have an annual cycle; so a mathematical adjustment is necessary depending on the time of year. The nocturnal, with movable dials, bypasses the need for calculation.

To make a nocturnal, trace the three shapes shown in Figure D onto stiff cardboard. Cut out the shapes, making a small hole in the center of each. Stack the pieces with the larger disk on the bottom, the smaller disk in the middle, and the pointer on top. Turn a threaded tube ⅜ inch in diameter and 1 inch long (available at hardware or electrical stores) through the center hole of all three. Cap both ends of the tube with nuts, but keep them loose enough so the dials can turn freely. Cut a 6-inch length of ⅜-inch dowel (available at hobby shops); then saw a groove ⅜ inch deep in one end. Use this groove to fasten the outermost dial to the dowel on the line that separates June from July. Secure it with white glue if necessary.

To use the nocturnal, align the triangular indicator (located between the 4 and 5 A.M. markers of the smaller dial) with the date on the larger dial. (The numbers 10 and 20 in each month's compartment represent those dates; other dates can be approximated.) Then hold the instrument at arm's length with the dowel handle pointing downward. Sight the North Star through the hole in the center tube, and swing the pointer until its longer edge is lined up with the Pointer Stars of the Big Dipper. The point where this edge crosses the smaller dial indicates the time. In the reading shown on page 2498, it is January 31, and the time is about 1:30 A.M.

When you compare your nocturnal reading with clock time, you may find a discrepancy, as with the noon mark (page 2493), again due to the use of standard time zones and daylight saving time. You can adjust the reading as described on page 2493 though you will not need to compensate for fluctuations in the sun cycle.

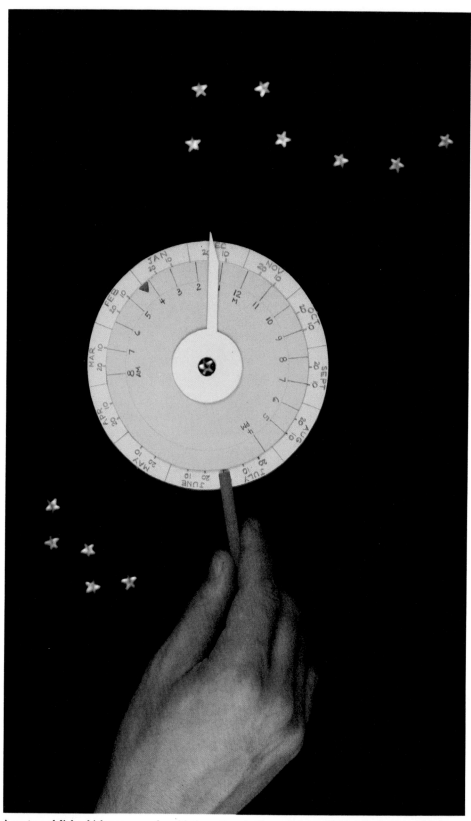

A nocturnal dial, which you can make with the pattern in Figure D (page 2497), tells the time with the help of the stars. An imaginary reading taken in front of a simulated sky shows how the dial is used. The red triangular marker on the time dial is aligned with the date (here, January 31) on the outer wheel. Then, with the dial held at arm's length, the North Star is sighted through the center hole and the long side of the yellow pointer is aimed at the Pointer Stars of the Big Dipper. The time is indicated where the pointer crosses the blue wheel, in this case about 1:30 A.M.

How Accurate Is Your Watch?

The stars are so reliable as time tellers that you can use them to check the accuracy of a watch or clock. To do this, you simply check when a star disappears on two successive nights. Stick a straight pin vertically into the sill or a rail of a western window. Select a nearby roof ridge to sight against, as shown in Figure E. If possible, choose a roof that appears well above the horizon as you view it beyond the pin head, because optical distortion and cloud interference are greatest near the horizon. Pick any bright star situated at that moment just above the roof line, and sighting the star with the pin head, watch it set below the roof. (Do not use the North Star, which alone remains stationary in the sky.) Record the exact moment—the hour, minute, and second—when the star drops out of sight. Make a diagram of the surrounding stars so you can find the same star again on the next night. Do not remove the pin.

On the next night, go to the window ten minutes earlier. Consult the diagram, if necessary, to locate the star previously used. Sight it as before with the pin head. As it sets behind the roof, note the exact time. Subtract this time from the time the star set the previous night. If you find it set 3 minutes and 56 seconds earlier the second time, you have a timepiece accurate to within one second per day. (The precise difference in setting time is 3 minutes, 55.90644 seconds per day.) If the difference between the recorded times is greater, your watch is fast by that much; if less, it is slower by that much.

For related projects and crafts, see "Astronomy," "Candlemaking," "Maps and Pathfinding," "Sundials," and "Weather Forecasting."

Ibis-headed Thoth, the Egyptian god of time, is said to have given man the calendar, as well as language, writing, and the social order. He was regarded both as the moon god and as the earthly representative of the sun god, Ra, who was supreme in the Egyptian pantheon. He holds the symbol of life in his left hand and in his right a stylus, for recording the fate in the afterlife of the souls of the dead.

E
Figure E: To check the accuracy of a clock or watch, record the exact moment when a star sets behind a neighbor's roof on two successive nights. Sight past a pin head, as illustrated, to keep your viewing angle the same on both nights. The star will set 3 minutes and 56 seconds earlier on the second night.

TIN AND PIERCED WORK
The Poorer Man's Silver

John Holochwost is a tinsmith in residence at Waterloo Village Restoration in Stanhope, New Jersey. He left his trade as a printer in order to restore old carriages. In time he acquired other skills in blacksmithing, pottery making, broom making, and tinsmithing. John's tinware designs include candlestands, pitchers, and ornaments.

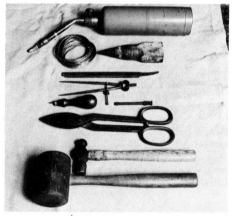

1: The basic tinsmithing tools you need for the projects on the following pages are, from top to bottom: a propane torch with a soldering tip; 50/50 (tin-to-lead ratio) solid-core solder; a pointed wooden stake; a metal file; a compass; an awl (left) and straight-edged punch (right); tin snips with straight-edged blades; a ball peen hammer; and a rubber mallet.

Shiny and inexpensive (or free), tin is an appealing craft material. Easy to cut and shape, lightweight and highly reflective, it makes useful lighting devices, ornaments, and household utensils with an old-time look. What is called tin, of course, contains only a small amount of pure tin in a coating over steel.

The history of the use of pure tin to improve other metals dates back to around 3000 B. C. when it was combined with copper to make an alloy, bronze, starting the period in history known as the Bronze Age. In 79 A. D., tin and lead were first alloyed to form solder, used for joining metals. During the Middle Ages another tin-lead alloy, pewter, was developed. Lustrous and tarnish resistant, pewter was used to imitate silver in church accessories and tableware, hence was nicknamed the poor man's silver. In the fourteenth century, tin was first used to plate thin iron sheets. The tin gave luster to the iron and protected it from corrosion; the iron gave strength to the tin. Even less expensive than pewter, tin-plated iron was quickly adopted for craft work. In the American colonies it was called the poorer man's silver.

Today, tin-plated steel is used in making items ranging from ball bearings to tin cans to musical instruments. With it, craftsmen can make objects that resemble colonial wares, such as cookie cutters (page 2502), a candle snuffer and sconce (page 2504), or a decorative fruit bowl (page 2508). To make these pieces, you can buy new sheets from roofing and plumbing suppliers, or you can simply recycle used tin cans.

Tools for Tinsmithing

To transfer a pattern for a tinware design, you will need: a pencil; a black felt-tipped marker with water-soluble ink or a grease pencil; a ruler; a compass; 18-by-24-inch sheets of tracing paper; masking tape; and newspapers. In addition, you will need these basic metalworking tools: a bench vise; a pair of 14-inch straight-bladed tin snips; an awl; a metal file; and double-thick cotton work gloves to protect your hands from the sharp edges. For bending and folding tin, you will need a small ball peen hammer; a mallet with a medium-sized leather or rubber head; a wooden stake sharpened at one end; and a garden spade or other piece of heavy metal with a straight, sharp edge. For soldering metal you will need: an asbestos pad; steel wool; a small jar of rosin flux; a natural-bristle watercolor brush; 50/50 (tin-to-lead ratio) solid-core solder; and an 80-watt electric soldering iron with an extension cord and stand, or a propane torch with a soldering tip (photograph 1). The additional materials needed are listed with the project instructions that follow.

Materials

Five 11-by-20-inch sheets of tin (actually tin-plated steel but commonly called tin) are all you need for all of the projects described on the following pages. The kind available at roofing and plumbing suppliers—.012 inch thick—is recommended. Or use empty gallon-sized tin cans, the kind used to hold institutional

Surrounded by a growing collection of old tin canisters and lanterns, John Holochwost reproduces such pieces as coffee tins and candle snuffers (foreground), reminiscent of a bygone era. He demonstrates tinsmithing techniques in the tin shop at Waterloo Village Restoration.

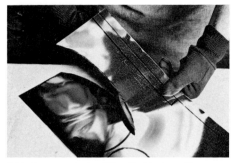

2: Before you start cutting the tin, transfer pattern outlines with a felt-tipped marker filled with water-soluble ink. Wearing double-thick cotton work gloves to protect your hands, cut just inside the pattern outlines with tin snips. Remove any guidelines that show on a cutout piece, using a damp rag.

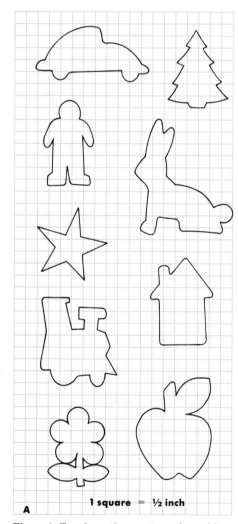

1 square = ½ inch

Figure A: To enlarge these patterns for cookie-cutter blades, draw a grid on an 18-by-24-inch sheet of paper, with each square measuring ½ inch. Copy the patterns onto the larger grid, transferring the lines one square at a time.

foods or oil. Often large cans of this size are given away free at service stations and restaurants. Even 32-ounce juice cans will do.

If you recycle a tin can, follow these steps to ready it for craft use. First, empty the can, and remove the label by soaking it in warm water. Wash the tin with hot, soapy water to remove any chemical residue or odor. Even cans used to hold solvents and paints can be used if you clean them thoroughly. Dry the can; then lightly rub the exterior with fine steel wool to remove any glue that remains and to polish the metal. Remove the top and bottom lids, including the rims, with a can opener. Then cut along the side seam, wearing heavy gloves and using tin snips. Separate the cut edges. To flatten the can, lay it convex side up on several thicknesses of newspaper, and pound it with a rubber mallet. Then you are ready to transfer a pattern to the metal sheet and cut out the pieces (photograph 2).

The blade of a tin cookie cutter can be bent into almost any shape to prepare eye-catching treats; four such shapes are pictured. Other kitchen utensils made of tin in colonial America were pie crimpers, basins, graters, ladles, skimmers, strainers, and teapots. During the 1800s there were so many peddlers selling tinware through the New England countryside that they were said to be as "thick [plentiful] as toads after a rain."

Jewelry, Lapidary, and Metalwork
Cookie cutters   ¢ ⊠ ⚹ ⚓

Tin-crafted cookie cutters shaped like the silhouettes of animals, flowers, houses, or stars, such as those shown above at left, were often hung around the hearth in the homes of colonial America. During the holiday season, neighbors would exchange cookie cutters and use them to make festive Christmas cookies. As shown, these shapes are useful cookie cutters. Made without handles, they could be used as tree ornaments, assembled into mobiles, or arranged over a fireplace or range.

One cautionary note: lead-bearing solder should not be used in any food utensil in a way that might let the solder contaminate food. Handles are soldered on these cookie cutters so the solder does not touch the cookie dough. In any event, according to the Bureau of Lead Poisoning Control, there is no danger; cookie dough is nonacidic and does not absorb lead.

For each cookie cutter, you need two strips of tin, one ¾ inch wide by 20 inches long for the cutter and one 2 inches wide by 10 inches long for the handle. You also need a 20-inch piece of cotton string for measuring. You could, of course, adjust the length of the cutter to match the amount of tin available. For example, the star pattern shown has ten 1½-inch edges, totaling 15 inches. If you have only a 10-inch strip of tin, make each edge 1 inch long. The handle should be 5 or 6 inches longer than the diameter of the shaped cutter.

3: To fold the edge of a piece of tin, first clamp a spade or other rigid and beveled piece of metal in a vise. Position the tin overlapping the rigid edge by the desired amount. Use a rubber mallet to hammer the edge into a right angle.

4: Flatten the bent edges by pounding them inward with a rubber mallet. To keep the outer surface free of scratches, pad the worktable with fabric or newspapers before hammering. This side is referred to as the hemmed edge.

5: To make the star cookie cutter, accordion-pleat the tin strip that will be the cutter into even segments, after you fold the top edge. Then open the cutter with your fingers. The top edge is folded to the outside of the star.

With pencil and ruler, enlarge the cookie-cutter shapes in Figure A. Lay the string around the edge of a pattern to determine the length of tin you need for the cutter. Wearing gloves to guard against cuts, use tin snips to trim the tin strip to the exact length needed.

To finish the side edges of the handle so you do not cut your hand, you need to fold the edges under. In the tin shop, I use a bar folder—a mechanical device that dates back to 1830. To accomplish the folding at home, clamp a spade (or other piece of rigid metal with a beveled, straight edge) in a bench vise, beveled edge on top. Put the handle strip lengthwise over the spade edge, overlapping it about ¼ inch. Starting at one end, bend the raw edge to a right angle by pounding it gently with a rubber mallet (photograph 3). Bend the opposite edge of the handle the same way. Then place the handle on a padded surface to protect it from scratches. Using the rubber mallet, flatten the bent edges (photograph 4). Use the same procedure to fold one long edge (the top edge) of the cutter.

To form the star-shaped cookie cutter, bend a 15-inch tin strip with one finished edge to make 1½-inch accordion folds, so you have ten sides of the same length. If you have excess tin on the last side, snip it off. Unfold the pleats to form the star (photograph 5). To shape any other cookie cutter, align one end of a tin strip with any corner or angle of the enlarged pattern. Keep the finished edge on top. Wearing gloves, bend and fold the metal as you follow the pattern outline.

The handle for each cookie cutter is a D shape, with the straight side slightly longer than the diameter of the cutter. To form the curved part of the D shape, put a broomstick or stake in a vise. Keeping the edge folds to the inside of the curve, bend the tin around the stake. Rest your thumbs on top of the metal with fingers underneath, and flex gently, gradually working the strip along the curve of the stake (photograph 6). Shape the metal into a neat J shape. Then sharply bend the straight section, the length of the cutter, to turn the J shape into an enclosed D shape, with a joint at one corner.

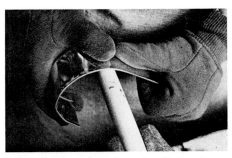

6: To curl a piece of metal to make a D shaped handle, bend it gradually around a broomstick or stake with your thumbs and fingers. Make a J shape, leaving enough uncurved tin to bend across the open side, enclosing the D shape.

7: To close a seam, first clean edges to be joined with steel wool and coat them with flux. When the soldering iron is hot, put on gloves, press the joint together, and apply a drop of solder at each end of the seam.

Soldering and Joining

Rub the cutter and handle lightly with fine steel wool to remove any grease that might keep solder from sticking. Rest the pieces on an asbestos pad, and brush a coat of flux onto the seams to be joined. Clean the tip of the soldering iron with steel wool and coat it with flux. Wearing gloves, plug in the soldering iron and rest it on its stand. Or follow the manufacturer's directions to light a propane torch with a soldering-tip attachment. Unwind some solder from the roll, wait a few minutes, then test to see if the iron is hot enough. It is ready when the tip of the iron, rubbed over the solder, makes it flow evenly. To solder, pick up a drop of solder with the iron and join each end of the handle seam (photograph 7). Let the solder cool for a few seconds before releasing pressure on the joint. As the solder cools, it will change from looking wet and shiny to looking dry and dull. Next, solder the joint in the cutter at the folded top edge. Then center the finished edge of the cutter on the flat side of the handle. Solder at four points where the two pieces touch to finish (photograph 8).

8: To finish a cookie cutter, center the soldered cutter on the flat side of the handle, making sure the folded edge of the cutter rests on the handle. Apply solder in about four spots to bond the cutter to the handle.

The cone-shaped candle snuffer (left) is a neater way to extinguish a flame than blowing it out and running the risk of spattering hot wax on a wall or table top. This device, invented centuries ago, can be hung from its looped handle next to a wall sconce such as the one shown here. A sconce with a reflector panel spreads the light from the flame to brighten any corner with a touch of colonial charm. A cupped bobèche under the candle catches wax drippings. A recycled tin can was pierced with an awl to make the lacy shade that lets candlelight radiate to walls and ceiling.

Jewelry, Lapidary, and Metalwork

Candle sconce and snuffer

In times past, when candles provided one of the main sources of illumination, the candle snuffer pictured above (left), was a useful household utensil. Consisting of a small cup at the end of a handle, it could be used to extinguish a candle with no danger of spattering hot wax.

The Snuffer
To make a candle snuffer, you need the tools in photograph 1 (page 2500). If you do not have a wooden stake, substitute a 1-inch dowel or broomstick handle about 18 inches long. Sharpen one end with a knife and rasp. In addition, you will need two pieces of tin, one ¾ inch wide and 10 inches long for the handle, the other 2¾ inches square for the cone, plus tracing paper for the patterns.

Shaping the Snuffer
Start by enlarging the patterns for the snuffer cone and handle (Figure B) on tracing paper. Cut out the patterns. Tape the cone pattern to the tin, aligning straight edges of the pattern with metal edges. Mark the curved edge on the tin, using a felt-tipped pen and water-soluble ink. Wearing gloves, use tin snips to cut out the shape, cutting just inside the line. Do the same with the handle.

9: To shape the cone of the candle snuffer, secure a pointed stake horizontally in a vise; then place the right-angle corner of the cone piece of tin at the tip of the stake. Use your fingers to wrap the metal around the point. Be sure to wear gloves.

10: Rest the cone on top of the stake and tap the tip closed, using the flat side of a ball peen hammer. This will narrow the opening in the side seam. Return the cone to the stake point, and tap it with a rubber mallet until the seam edges overlap by ⅜ inch.

11: To loop the snuffer handle, clamp a broomstick horizontally in a vise. Overlap it with one end of the handle by about 1 inch, with the folded edge on top. Tap the handle with a mallet as you move it over the broomstick until a closed 1-inch loop is formed.

Secure the stake horizontally in the vise. Use your fingers to shape the metal cone around the pointed end (photograph 9). Then remove the cone and rest it on top of the stake. Close the tip of the cone by gently tapping it with the flat side of a ball peen hammer (photograph 10). Then slide the cone back over the stake point and close the joining edges by overlapping them and flattening them with a rubber mallet. When the cone is finished, use tin snips to trim off any unevenness along the rim. Set the cone aside while you make the handle.

Folding and Curling the Handle

As described on page 2503, use a spade edge and rubber mallet to fold in a ¼-inch-wide hem along each long edge of the metal strip you cut for the handle. The sharp edges will nearly meet along the center of the handle's length. So that you can grip the handle with a forefinger or hang it on a hook, curl one end of the handle into a loop. Clamp a broomstick in the vise horizontally and hold the handle against it, folded edges down. Let one end overlap the broomstick about an inch. Use a rubber mallet to tap this end of the handle to curve it around the broomstick, supporting the rest of the strip with the other hand (photograph 11). Keep sliding the handle forward as you tap until you close the loop.

Place the handle, folded edges up, on top of the worktable, and extend the end opposite the loop ¼ inch over the edge of the table. Use a rubber mallet to bend the projecting tab down to an angle of about 80 degrees, slightly less than a right angle (photograph 12). Follow the instructions for soldering and joining (page 2503) to close the seam along the side of the cone. Fit the handle tab against the side of the cone with the angle even with the rim. Then solder the handle to the cone along the seam.

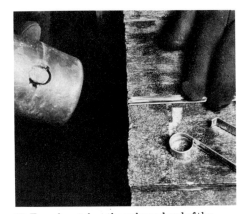

12: To make a tab at the unlooped end of the handle, place it on the worktable with the folded side on top, extending ¼ inch over the edge. Use a rubber mallet to bend this end, forming an 80-degree angle. This tab should be flat with the rim of the candle-snuffer cone.

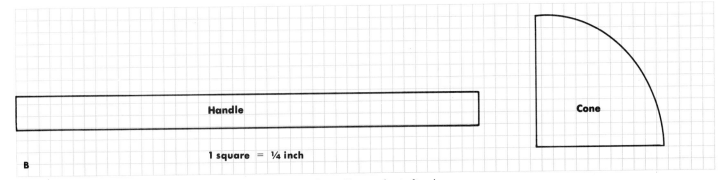

Handle

Cone

1 square = ¼ inch

B

Figure B: Enlarge these patterns for the cone and handle of the candle snuffer on a sheet of tracing paper ruled with ¼-inch squares. Transfer the patterns, one square at a time, onto the larger grid; then cut out the tracings. Use the cutouts to outline the pieces on the tin with a felt-tipped pen having water-soluble ink.

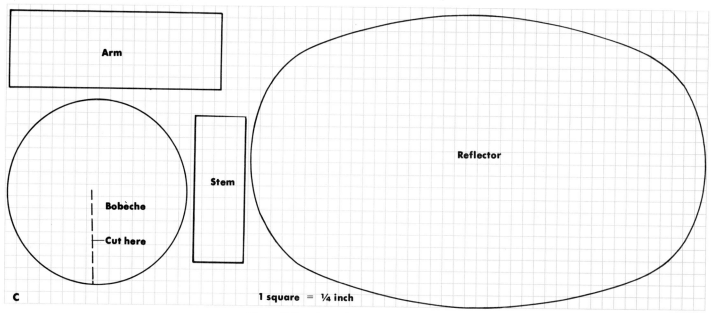

1 square = ¼ inch

Figure C: To enlarge these patterns for the sconce parts, draw a ¼-inch grid on an 18-by-24-inch sheet of paper. Copy the patterns one square at a time until you have transferred all the lines onto the larger grid.

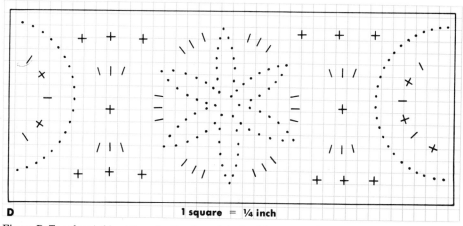

1 square = ¼ inch

Figure D: To enlarge this pattern for the pierced shade of the sconce, draw a ¼-inch grid on a 4-by-10-inch sheet of paper. Then transfer the pattern to the larger grid, one square at a time.

The Sconce

Tin is such a good reflector that it can magnify a single flame enough to light a room. A favorite early illuminator was the decorative wall bracket called a sconce, such as the one shown on page 2504. The sheet of tin attached to the sconce behind the candle magnifies its light. Alternatively, to shelter the flame from drafts, a pierced tin shade can be placed over the candle. The holes in the shade make light patterns on the walls and ceilings.

To make the sconce pictured, you need an 11-by-20-inch sheet of tin or a flattened gallon-size can and the tinsmithing tools listed on page 2500. For piercing the tin shade, you need an awl, nails ⅛ inch in diameter, and a screwdriver with a 3/16-inch-wide tip. In addition, you need: an empty 16-ounce can for the shade (save the top); a small jar of flat-finish acrylic white paint; a small nylon paintbrush; two pounds of sand; and a 5-inch-tall candle 1 inch in diameter.

Enlarge the patterns for the sconce on paper ruled in ¼-inch squares (Figure C). Cut out the pieces and arrange them on the tin. With a felt-tipped pen or grease pencil, outline the pieces on the metal.

Wearing gloves, cut the shapes from the tin with tin snips. Clamp a spade with a straight, beveled edge in a vise. Fold in ¼ inch on both long edges of the arm and ¼ inch on one edge of the candle stem, following the directions on page

13: To curve the reflector, center it lengthwise over the broomstick. Gently press the side edges toward each other until the middle of the reflector is ¾ inch deep. The curved metal will disperse the reflection of the candlelight.

14: After you have cut out the bobèche that will catch wax drippings, use tin snips to make a cut from the edge to the center. Press the edges of the disk together until they overlap, forming a shallow cup.

15: To make a pierced design in the candle shade, tape the pattern (Figure D) around a sand-filled can. Use a hammer to tap the piercing instrument—awl, nail, or screwdriver—until it pierces the side of the can.

2503. Replace the spade with a broomstick held horizontally in the vise. Wrap the candle stem around it with the folded edge facing out. Shape the stem into a 1-inch-wide loop, following the instructions on page 2503. Position the arm, folded edge on the bottom, over the broomstick. Beginning at one end, gradually pull the metal over the broomstick until it forms a wide U shape. One-half inch from one end of the arm, bend the metal back at a 45-degree angle to form the tab that will support the bobèche, the collar that catches candle drippings.

To shape the reflector, center the oval-shaped piece of tin lengthwise on top of the broomstick. Lightly roll the metal over the broomstick, pressing the long edges toward each other until the middle of the front surface is indented about ¾ inch (photograph 13). Using a nail, pierce a ⅛-inch hole centered in the reflector ¾ inch from its top edge. This will be used for hanging the sconce.

To form the bobèche, use tin snips to make a straight cut from the edge of the tin disk to its center (indicated by the dashed cutting line in Figure C). Press the cut edges together until they overlap ⅜ inch (photograph 14), making a shallow cone.

Piercing the Shade

Remove all labels from the can that you will use for the shade, and rinse it in hot water. Dry the can. Then apply a thin coat of white paint to the inside and set the can aside to dry. Enlarge the pattern for the shade (Figure D); then wrap it around the can, making sure the top edge of the pattern lines up with the top rim of the can. Tape the pattern in place. Fill the can with sand and replace the top lid, taping it in place.

Cover the worktable with newspapers, rest the can on its side, and assemble the piercing tools. To make round holes, use an awl or ice pick. For straight lines use the screwdriver. To pierce the metal, hold the tool against the can and tap it with a hammer until the metal is penetrated (photograph 15). The sand keeps the can from caving in. Once all the holes are pierced, remove the tracing, the top lid, and the sand; then remove the bottom with a can opener.

Joining the Parts

To assemble the four pieces of the sconce, follow the instructions for soldering and joining on page 2503 and refer to Figure E. To begin, solder a ¾-inch section of the straight end of the arm to the back of the reflector. Solder edges of the arm to ensure a secure bond. Place the candle stem, with its folded edge on top, in the middle of the bobèche. Align the seam lines and solder the bottom edge of the candle stem to the bobèche. Rest the reflector on its back. With the seam of the bobèche lined up with the middle of the reflector, position the arm tab 1¾ inches down from the front rim of the bobèche. This should leave a ¾-inch space between the bobèche and the face of the reflector. Solder each edge of the arm tab to the bobèche.

Using the hole in the reflector, hang the sconce from an upholstery nail. Put the candle in the candle stem. Light the candle and cover it with the pierced shade, resting the shade on the bobèche.

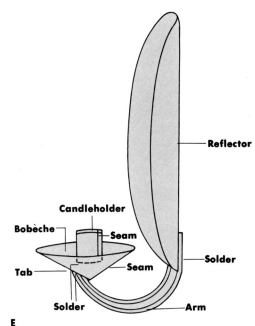

E

Figure E: This diagram indicates the points to solder when you assemble the sconce. Center and solder the flat edge of the arm to the back of the reflector, ¾ inch from its bottom edge. Solder the unfinished bottom edge of the candle stem to the middle of the bobèche. Solder the bent tab of the arm to the underside of the bobèche, just in front of its center point.

Decorative fruit takes on a festive look in a gleaming tinware centerpiece. This design, consisting of four curved side panels that lock into a square base, is not difficult to make once you have mastered basic tinsmithing techniques.

Jewelry, Lapidary, and Metalwork
Fruit bowl

Once you have mastered the techniques of cutting, folding, shaping, and soldering tin, as described on the preceding pages, you will be able to make pieces like the centerpiece bowl shown above. It has a square bottom and four curved side panels that interlock like a puzzle. In addition to the tools listed on page 2500, you will need two 11-by-20-inch sheets of tin and a curved form such as a garden shovel with a rounded blade or the lid from an empty gallon can.

With pencil and ruler, enlarge the patterns for the bottom and side panel of the fruit bowl (Figure F). Cut out the patterns and arrange them on tin; then trace around them with a grease pencil. Trace the side panel four times. Wearing gloves, cut out the pieces with tin snips. The side panels must fit together precisely; so cut carefully just inside the pattern lines.

Using the garden shovel or can lid as a form, shape the top edge of each side panel. Lock the form in a vise. If you use a shovel, have the convex side facing you. Holding a side panel so the tab is on the right and the curved edge is on top, align it with a similar curve in the form. Then raise the side panel until its top edge overlaps the form by ⅛ inch.

Press the bottom of the panel against the form to keep it from slipping as you tap the top edge over the rounded form with a rubber mallet. Bend the entire top edge back ⅛ inch. Then place the panel with its bent edge up on a padded surface. Flatten the folded edge with a rubber mallet. Put a straight-edged spade in the vise. Hold the panel lengthwise in front of the spade so the curved edge is on the bottom and the fold is in the back. Overlap ½ inch of the bottom edge over the spade.

Use a rubber mallet to bend the metal to a 45-degree angle along the bottom edge, as indicated by the blue dotted line in Figure F. Turn the panel over and make a similar fold ¼ inch down from the same bottom edge, as shown by the red dotted line in Figure F. Turn the panel over and use a rubber mallet to hammer the ¼-inch fold nearly closed. (Take care that the ½-inch fold remains in a 45-degree angle to the front of the panel.) Using the spade and mallet, bend the side tab forward so it forms a right angle. Clamp a broom handle in the vise and curl the top edge of each side panel back, following the instructions for shaping the oval reflector of the sconce (page 2507). Keep the folded edge facing away from you, and curve only the top 1½ inches. The curve should be no more than ½ inch deep. Repeat these steps in the same way for the other side panels.

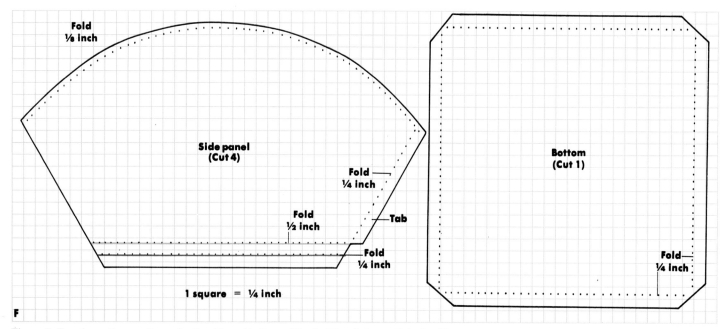

Figure F: To enlarge these patterns for the side and bottom of the fruit bowl, draw a ¼-inch grid on an 18-by-24-inch sheet of paper. Copy the patterns, one square at a time, onto the larger grid.

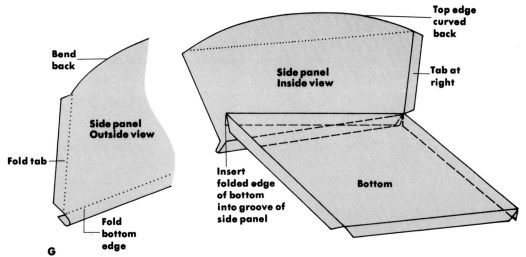

Figure G: The pieces of the fruit bowl are interlocked by inserting the flaps of the square bottom piece into the folded groove at the bottom of each side panel. The sides are joined by butting the straight left-hand edge of one panel within the corner of the folded right-hand edge of an adjacent panel. To strengthen the design, solder is applied at random along the corner seams.

To make the bottom of the bowl, fold the four side tabs to form right angles. These hook into the channels at the bottom of each side panel (Figure G). Use the spade and the rubber mallet.

To assemble the fruit bowl, fit the left edge of a side panel snugly into a tab at the right edge of another side panel, as shown in the color photograph on page 2501. Solder this joint, as described on page 2503. One at a time, fit and solder the remaining side panels together. Set the fruit bowl upright on the workbench and insert the bottom so its tabs fit snugly into the channels of the side piece. Then solder the corners of the side pieces. Also solder the side joints together for extra strength. According to the Bureau of Lead Poisoning Control, there is no danger that the solder will contaminate the fruit.

For related entries, see "Colonial Crafts," "Lamps and Shades," "Mobiles," "Pewtersmithing," "Repoussé and Chased Metal," "Silversmithing," "Tin Painting," and "Wire Sculpture."

TIN PAINTING
Prettying Up the Wares

For 25 years, Gen Ventrone has taught, lectured, and written about the art of Early American decorating, including tin painting. Her methods proved so successful that she appeared in a television series, The Tin Lady, *prepared for distribution by National Educational Television.*

In the days before tableware and kitchenware were mass-produced, painting tinware by hand was a significant occupation. Professionals usually worked with local whitesmiths, as tinsmiths were known, decorating their line of trays, pitchers, snuffboxes, pots, bread boxes, and trays. Proper young ladies were taught a refined version of the art, widely known as japanning after its distant oriental origin. Country folk, notably the Pennsylvania Dutch, developed unique regional styles.

The motifs used in tin painting were frequently fruits, flowers, birds, and patriotic symbols, applied either freehand or with stencils. Abstract ornamentation, using combinations of brushstrokes to create rhythmic patterns, were also popular. To set off the design, the tinware was first painted a dark color—usually black. The design itself was executed in a variety of traditional colors, including metallic gold, silver, and bronze.

Though the trade disappeared in the latter part of the nineteenth century, its secrets were not lost. As the following projects indicate, tin painting is still an enjoyable craft for many.

Above: Authentic Early American designs, such as the one barely discernible on the old box on the left, can be used as the inspiration for painting a new box (right). Gen Ventrone often restores old tin objects to their former beauty by repainting the design right on the original piece.

Opposite: These pieces from Gen Ventrone's collection of painted tin are decorated with three different techniques. Country tin painting can be identified by its red, green, and yellow designs painted with freehand brushstrokes. Freehand bronze work, a technique that involves rubbing bronze powders onto a tacky surface, was used on the document box in the foreground. Antique stenciling is represented by the elaborately decorated tray in the background; with this technique, fine bronze powders are applied to a tacky surface through a stencil.

Suggested reading
Early American Decorating Techniques by Mariette Paine Slayton, the Macmillan Company, New York.

Early American Decoration by Esther Stevens Brazer (out of print; available at libraries).

Early American Stencils on Walls and Furniture by Janet Waring, Peter Smith, Gloucester, Mass.

Suppliers of tin-painting equipment
Supplies can often be purchased at paint stores or art stores, especially those that cater to signpainters. Or they can be ordered by mail from:

Arthur Brown & Bros. Inc., 2 West 46th St., New York, N.Y. 10036

Brenner's Paint Shop, 8 Samoset St., Plymouth, Mass. 02360

Carson and Ellis, Inc., 1153 Warwick Ave., Warwick, R.I. 02888 (send for catalogue)

Crafts Manufacturing Co., 72 Massachusetts Ave., Lunenburg, Mass. 01462 (send for catalogue)

CRAFTNOTES: PREPARING AND FINISHING A TIN SURFACE

Before you begin to decorate anything made of metal, the surface needs preparation. Then, after you have completed painting the design, you should finish the surface to protect the design and to impart a soft, satiny sheen. For all three of the tin-painting techniques described on these pages—country tin, freehand bronze, and antique stenciling—the preparation and finishing stages are essentially the same.

Preparing the surface
The left half of the old tin tray pictured above has been prepared for decoration, while the right half is still in its original condition, showing the change that can be achieved. To prepare the metal for decorating you will need: oil-based flat black paint; rust inhibitor; a ½-inch paintbrush; and a fine grade of sandpaper.

The first step is cleaning the surface. If the metal is new, rub the surface with fine sandpaper to give it a slight texture that will hold paint well. If the metal is old, remove any paint with paint remover. If the piece is rusty, take off the rust with sandpaper, brushing away the rust particles with a dry brush.

Next, brush on one coat of rust inhibitor on all sides. After 24 hours, sand down any ridges. Apply a second coat of rust inhibitor; let dry for 24 hours, and sand smooth again.

After applying at least two coats of rust inhibitor—more if necessary to achieve a smooth, uniform coverage—brush a coat of flat black oil-based paint on all surfaces. Let it dry for 24 hours; then sand lightly with very fine sandpaper. Repeat the painting, drying, and sanding steps a second time and the metal should be ready for decorating as described in the project instructions.

Finishing the surface
To finish a decorated surface, you will need: varnish; a 1½-inch paintbrush with soft natural or synthetic bristles; wet-and-dry sandpaper (No. 600); raw linseed oil; rottenstone (a polishing material available at hardware stores); vinegar; household ammonia; and a pure bristle rubbing brush (a piece of felt from a man's hat is a good substitute).

Wipe away all dust; then coat all surfaces with varnish. Let dry for 24 hours. Dip the sandpaper in water or put a few drops of water on the varnished tin surface. Rub the entire surface gently with circular motions, doing a small section at a time (above). Be careful not to cut through the varnish, especially over design areas.

Wash with soapy water to remove any sanding residue and dry thoroughly. Apply another coat of varnish, let dry for 24 hours, wet-sand it, and wash with soapy water. Repeat this procedure as many times as necessary to achieve a very smooth surface.

To achieve the desired satin finish, make a paste of powdered rottenstone and linseed oil, adding just a dash of vinegar and a dash of household ammonia. Rub this paste over the surface with the rubbing brush or piece of felt, again using a circular motion (above). As you rub the entire surface, in time you will create a fine, satiny patina that gives the metal the appearance of a well-preserved antique.

1: The tin-painting supplies shown are (left to right): a tube of oil paint, palette knife, India ink, sword-striper brush, three square-tipped quill brushes, silver pencil, crow-quill pen and pen point, and a stylus, all on a disposable paper palette. At the top are a bottle of paint thinner and a block of magnesia; to the right is a roll of frosted acetate.

This tray is decorated with an authentic Early American design in a style called country tin painting. All the brushstrokes are done freehand, following a pattern. This is a relatively simple design, suitable for many uses.

Paint and Color
Country tin painting

Country tin painting is the simplest form of this decorative art, and it is the place to begin. The work is accomplished with simple brushstrokes. While they are not complicated, they do require much practice to perfect. Even gifted artists will make many practice strokes before beginning work on a piece. Skillfully applied tin ornamentation is perfectly flat, not raised or lumpy in appearance, and that is the effect the craftsman seeks.

Materials
The list of materials needed may seem overwhelming, but most are not costly and will last through several projects.

Oil paint in tubes: alizarin crimson, Prussian blue, raw umber, burnt umber, and Indian yellow or yellow lake (all transparent); titanium white and yellow ocher (both semitransparent); *japan oil paints:* chrome yellow or medium yellow, and American vermilion or signwriter's red (all opaque). The latter colors are commonly sold in half-pint cans. Each can has a layer of oil on top of pigment to keep it fresh. Dig under the oil with a palette knife for whatever pigment you need.

Occasionally you will want to mix colors to obtain a specific shade. For country yellow, mix japan medium yellow with raw umber. For country green, add Prussian blue to country yellow. For pink, add a bit of raw umber and signwriter's red to white. For light blue, add a bit of raw umber and Prussian blue to white. For Sheraton blue, add a bit of yellow ocher to light blue to obtain a green-blue. For salmon pink, add signwriter's red and yellow ocher to white.

Brushes: you need three square-tipped quills, also known as lettering brushes, or French quills, sizes 1, 2, and 3. The brush hairs should be ¾ inch long. You will also need a sword-striper brush, No. 0 or No. 00.

Instead of using turpentine for cleaning up, use paint thinner, sub-turps, or mineral spirits. They are less expensive. Keep a small amount in a can or bottle for cleaning brushes.

2513

A

Figure A: By mastering these few brushstrokes, you can paint all the shapes used in country tin painting. At top are right and left C shapes. Directly above to the right are S shapes and a rickrack line. At left, basic strokes are combined to make the flower, fruit, and leaf shapes. Below left are teardrops and thick and thin straight lines.

Clear glossy spar varnish is used as the medium and as a protective overlay for this work. Divide a half-pint can of the varnish into several small screw-top bottles and use one bottle at a time for the medium. Leave the rest in the can to use as a protective finish. Keep all containers tightly closed and upside down to keep the varnish fresh for a long period.

Miscellaneous: you need a 12-inch-square piece of window glass for practicing strokes; masking tape; India ink; crow-quill pen and point; a sharp-pointed colored pencil (silver-colored works best); tracing paper; a block of magnesia (available at drugstores); fine-point stylus (available at stationery stores); palette knife; paper palette; sheets of frosted acetate.

Other items often available in the home are: ruler; bottle caps; notebook (optional); scissors; pencil; cardboard; screw-top bottles; toilet tissue for clean-up. (Rags should not be used as they leave lint on the surface.) See Craftnotes, page 2512, for additional materials needed to prepare and finish the tin surface.

The Basic Brushstrokes

Study the illustrated brushstrokes (Figure A). There are two ways to master them—working freehand or working over tracings.

For the timid: trace the illustrated brushstrokes on a piece of tracing paper, using the crow-quill pen and India ink. Mount the tracing paper on a flat piece of cardboard slightly larger than the paper, using masking tape to hold each corner. Place the square of glass over the tracings and practice painting on the glass, using the tracings as a guide.

For the brave: you will not need tracings. Just follow the instructions as you copy the strokes when you practice on the glass. The strokes will look less stiff if they are made freehand.

First read the directions that follow; then practice the strokes.

Place a small amount of red japan pigment on your palette, and a small amount of varnish in a bottle cap. Have paint thinner handy to rinse and clean the brush.

Dip your brush into the varnish, then into the paint. Dress the brush on your palette; that is, brush back and forth to mix the paint and varnish to an enamel consistency. Too much varnish will make the paint transparent, too little will make the brush drag.

The C-shaped strokes are the easiest to learn; so do those first. Decide which direction is easier for you and practice that one first. Some people like to start with the C that goes to the right, others begin with the reverse C. When one seems easy

2: To begin making a C stroke, lay the paint-filled brush down on its flat side. It will ease into a round head.

3: Then draw the brush toward you quickly to the left or right, lifting gradually for the duration of the stroke. Do not twist the brush.

4: As you continue to lift and draw the brush toward you, it will come up to a fine hair line. Practice this stroke curved in both directions.

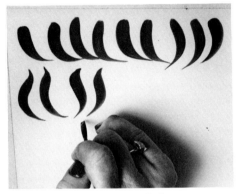

5: The S stroke is made in much the same way as the C stroke, but gradually becomes thick, and then diminishes to a thin hair line again.

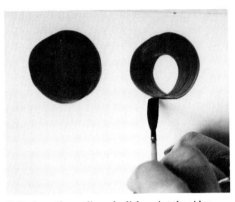

6: To form the outline of a disk, paint the sides with two C strokes, so the two strokes meet in the center at top and bottom.

7: To complete the disk, fill in the center with an S stroke. If you still have space to fill, add smaller strokes, but don't dab or the surface may get lumpy.

to make, practice the other.

To make the C-shaped stroke, follow photographs 2 through 4. The flatter you put the brush down at the beginning of the stroke, the wider it will be. To make smaller strokes, lay the brush down with less pressure. Hold the brush as you would hold a pencil, and let your hand glide freely on the little finger. Avoid twisting the brush; that would spoil the stroke.

The S stroke begins on the thin or knife edge of the brush. Fill the brush with varnish and paint as before. Touch the brush to the glass with the thin side facing you; then draw the brush toward you as you lay it down on the glass as you did in the C stroke, lifting slowly to execute the fine tail (photograph 5).

A combination of these brushstrokes is used to make the flower, the fruit, and the leaf. Practice painting a disk on the glass, stroking smoothly and avoiding dabs (photographs 6 and 7).

Begin the teardrop strokes with the thin side of the brush as well, but push the brush down as you draw it toward you to get the width you wish; then lift it to a fine tail. The harder you push the brush down, the wider the stroke.

The chain or rickrack stroke is made with a continuous up and down motion of the brush, without ever lifting it off the glass.

To paint stems and similar thin lines, hold the brush straight up with its thin side facing you, and pull quickly along the line toward you, using no pressure. Look at your practice strokes critically; wipe the glass clean with toilet tissue and paint thinner, then begin again.

When you are satisfied that you can make these strokes smoothly and consistently, try painting the simple tray design pictured on page 2513. All the designs on these pages are adapted from American tinware decorated in the early 1800s.

Prepare the tin surface as described in the Craftnotes, page 2512. Then trace the full-sized design (Figure B, page 2516). This basic design is shown without over strokes. Trace all of it, using the crow-quill pen and India ink on tracing paper.

B
Figure B: To make a pattern for the country tin painting on the tray shown on page 2513, trace this full-sized basic design. Practice executing it on an acetate overlay before you begin the actual tin decorating.

C
Figure C: After the basic red-and-green design is dry, add the yellow strokes and dots. Then, with pigment carried on only one side of the brush, paint the yellow over strokes on the fruit and leaves so the color shades away toward the center.

D
Figure D: When you have finished the yellow over strokes, use the same technique to paint the dark over strokes on the other side of the fruit—for a three-dimensional effect. Again put pigment on only one side of the brush.

Practicing the Design

Practicing the design on frosted acetate gives you an additional chance to learn the needed techniques. Attach the tracing of Figure B onto cardboard with masking tape; then place a piece of the acetate over it, frosted side up, and hold the corners down with masking tape while you paint. The acetate also provides a permanent record of the design, in case you want to duplicate it in the future.

To paint the fruit in this design, start by mixing red japan paint and varnish as you did for the practice brushstroke. Paint the large pieces first, then the smaller ones, all with red, using C and S strokes.

If you make a mistake, wipe the paint off with paint thinner and toilet tissue. If the thinner doesn't remove all the color, use a bit of carbon tetrachloride, being careful not to inhale the fumes. (Always work in a well-ventilated room and be aware of the fire hazard in these materials.)

When the red fruit has been painted to your satisfaction, set the acetate aside and let the paint dry for 24 hours. The next day, mix country green (page 2513). Practice a few strokes on glass. When the results please you, do all the green strokes in the design on acetate, and set it aside once more to dry for 24 hours.

The next day, mix a small amount of country yellow and paint all the yellow strokes and the dots between fruits, as well as the yellow over strokes (Figure C).

To paint the over strokes, first dress the brush with varnish. Then stroke the brush back and forth against the yellow pigment mixture so the color is picked up only on one side of the brush. Stroke that yellow, one-sided brush over the fruit so the yellow pigment will be heavy near the outer edge of the fruit and shade away to nothing toward the center.

Next, do the same thing with the dark shading on the fruit (Figure D). This time put a small amount of alizarin crimson on the palette and mix in a bit of burnt umber to tone it down. Dress the brush with varnish, pick up a bit of color on one side of the

2516

8: After applying magnesia to the back of the tracing, use the heel of your hand to rub off the excess magnesia. Enough powder will remain to enable you to use the pattern several times.

9: Position the tracing on the tin surface, powder-side down. Then go over the lines of the design with a stylus or dry ball-point pen. (Here, the design is being applied on a small canister.)

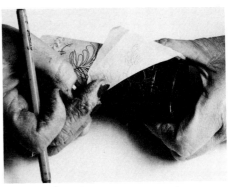

10: The magnesia will act as white carbon paper. When you have traced over all the outlines of the design, they will show clearly in white on the black-painted tin surface.

brush, and do the strokes over the fruit. Again, place the color-laden side of the brush toward the edge of the fruit so the color shades away to nothing toward the center. Let the finished design dry for 24 hours. Now you are ready to decorate the tray (or whatever other piece of tinware you have prepared).

Painting the Tray

To transfer the traced design to the tin surface, use magnesia and a stylus or dry ball-point pen as shown in photographs 8 through 10. (The tin's surface must be prepared in advance, as detailed in the Craftnotes, page 2512.) Remove the tracing paper carefully. Then paint the design on the tray as you did on acetate. Paint the red fruit first, then green leaves, then the solid yellow strokes, allowing 24 hours of drying time after each color. Do not paint the over strokes yet.

When the basic design is dry, dust the tray with a cloth dampened with paint thinner. Now mark where you will place stripes to border the design. Tray stripes are traditionally applied in three rows, the first about ⅛ inch in from where the gallery, or rim, joins the flat surface of the tray, then on the gallery about ⅛ inch up from the joining, and finally ⅛ inch below the edge of the tray.

Striping seems more difficult than it is. Use a ruler and silver pencil to mark where you will paint stripes. Then varnish the entire front of the tray, covering the basic design and the silver-pencil marks. If you varnish over the basic design, you will be able to correct subsequent errors by wiping them away.

Let the varnish dry for 24 hours; then apply the over strokes as you did on acetate. First paint the yellow strokes, then those that are dark red.

When the over strokes are dry, you are ready to do the striping. Mix country yellow and add varnish to it, blending the mixture with your palette knife until the paint is spreadable but not runny. To apply the stripe, use a sword-striper brush, practicing first on glass. Dress the sword-striper in the country-yellow paint mixture. Put some talcum powder on your little finger so it will slide easily. Holding the striper with thumb and forefinger, place your little finger against the edge of the glass and start to paint. (If the edge of the glass is sharp, cover it with masking tape.) Never look back, only watch where you are going. Place the knife edge of the striper on the glass and pull it toward you quickly (photograph 11), using your little finger against the edge of the glass as the guide to keep the line straight. Even if you can't draw a straight line, with practice you will be able to paint a good stripe. The flatter the brush is held, the wider that stripe will be; so if you want a narrow stripe, keep the brush high.

Now stripe the tray as you did the glass. Position the tray so that when you begin to paint, your little finger, talcum-powdered as before, will be guided by the edge of the gallery. Delicately press the sword-striper brush against the silver-pencil line and begin to paint. If the tray has rounded corners, do the straight striping first; then go back and join the corners, holding the striper high so you are using just the tip (photograph 12). Allow a day for the tray to dry. You are now ready to do the finishing, ending with a patina that will make the tray look antique, as described in the Craftnotes, page 2512.

11: Before you begin to paint the stripes on your tinware, practice on a piece of glass. Edges of the glass are encased with masking tape so the guiding finger can slide along the edges.

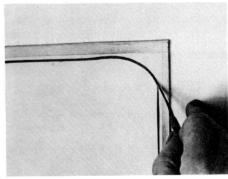

12: To form a rounded corner stripe on a tray, do the straight stripes first, then join them freehand at each corner.

This old tin canister is just waiting to be transformed with paint, but first the surface must be prepared as directed in the Craftnotes on page 2512.

Country tin painting can be done on curved surfaces as well as flat ones, as this canister shows. This is an adaptable design that can be doubled and quadrupled to fit whatever the size and shape of the area you wish to decorate.

Paint and Color
Canister

As your tin-painting skills develop, you will find yourself ready for more complicated designs. An advanced design for country tin painting is shown at lower left. To make it, you apply dark red over strokes, then white over strokes over the red. This versatile design can be used to encircle a canister, or it can be cut in half for decorating a smaller surface. It could also be doubled, should you want to decorate something large such as a milk can, or it could be repeated in series to make a large border design.

As explained on page 2516, trace the basic design (Figure E) onto tracing paper, and practice painting it on frosted acetate. First paint the basic design, using country red, letting it dry, then using country green. When it is dry, you are ready to apply the dark over strokes (Figure F). Mix alizarin crimson and burnt umber, load only one side of the brush, and paint the three dark leaflike areas in the center of each flower. Paint one side with the dark edge of the brush to the outside. Lift the brush, turn it over, and paint the other side of the leaf, bringing each stroke to a point. Paint three such shapes on each large flower. Next, again with the alizarin crimson-and-burnt umber mixture on one side of the brush, put a dark stroke on the outside edge of each petal, shading away toward the center.

Since varnish is the medium that carries the pigment (page 2514), you must dress the brush with varnish each time you need to pick up more paint. Pick up varnish, then the alizarin crimson-and-burnt umber mixture, and put a dark stroke on the right side of each bud, with the darkest part of the stroke to the outside of the bud. Using just the tip of a corner of the brush, put a dark-red dot on each of the small circles (berries). Let dry for 24 hours.

When the dark color is dry, apply the white over strokes (Figure G). Place some titanium white on the palette, and some varnish in a bottle cap. Dress the brush with varnish; then pick up some white on one side of the brush. Place a sheet of colored paper under the practice glass while you practice the transparent white stroke, making sure it is white on one side and fades on the other. When you are satisfied, do the white over strokes in the center of the dark leaflike areas. Do the stroke on one side, lift and turn the brush over, and do the stroke on the other side of each shape. Keep the white inside the dark crimson strokes, as pictured. On the left side of each bud, place a shaded white stroke with the heaviest white of the stroke to the outside, shading away toward the center of each bud.

To paint the white shapes at the bottom of each large flower, mix a bit of white with varnish and brush it out on the palette until it is almost dry. Using the knife edge of the brush, paint the five short white strokes at the bottom of each flower, starting at the bottom and drawing upward. Also paint the three leaf-like shapes with veinlike white lines inside. Then add the yellow over strokes on the leaves and let dry.

Design Modifications

If the acetate painting pleases you, transfer the design to the prepared tin surface (page 2517) and paint it. This design can be used alone, to fill a large, square area, or as a border (photograph 13). To make either modification, you need a second tracing that reverses the design so you can put the two together as shown.

It is not difficult to adapt a design to make it fit any area. Use a piece of tracing paper to outline the space to be decorated. Within that outline, trace the design, shifting the paper as necessary to make it fit and enlarging or reducing the spaces between elements as required. You may want to add brushstrokes not in the original design, such as the extra leaves in the square design (photograph 13).

Usually the striping on a milk can or canister is placed at the top and bottom of the main section of the design and around the lid. If you decorate a round object with a handle, such as a coffee pot, draw a stripe on each side of the handle as well.

Black is the easiest background color to use, but many favor other base colors such as old red or light blue. If you would like to experiment, paint a piece of cardboard with any background color that appeals to you. Put the cardboard under the glass while you try design colors on the glass to see how they look.

E

Figure E: To make a pattern for the advanced country tin painting shown on the canister opposite, trace this full-sized basic design. Practice painting this design on frosted acetate first. Then transfer the design to the metal surface you wish to decorate, as shown on page 2517, repeating or arranging the motif according to the size and shape of the space being painted.

F

Figure F: Use this as your guide when you add the dark-red over strokes to the basic design, thus shading the flowers and buds.

G

Figure G: When the dark-red strokes are dry, add white over strokes to the flowers and buds, and yellow over strokes to the leaves.

13: The single motif shown in Figure E can be modified for use as a border by repeating the pattern (left). To fill a large square area, the motif can be arranged as shown above right.

Gold-colored bronze powder, rubbed onto a design that has been painted with black enamel and then allowed to become tacky, makes an elegant freehand bronze design. The fine black line details have been etched in the powder-covered areas. Transparent art paint (burnt umber or burnt sienna) provides the shading.

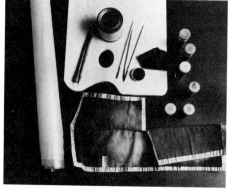

14: Supplies needed for freehand bronze painting include bronze powders in plastic vials (right); a velvet palette to hold the powders (bottom); frosted acetate for practicing (left); and, left to right on the paper palette, etching tool, stylus, can of black seal (or black enamel), square tipped quill brushes, and a small square of velvet for dusting the powders onto the tacky paint.

Paint and Color

Freehand bronze design

Once the basic brushstrokes of country tin painting are mastered (page 2514), a new challenge awaits you in freehand bronze work, called *chinoiserie* after its Chinese origin. These designs are usually made with gold-colored bronzing powder. They sometimes have etched lines that let the background color show through, or lines painted on the gold design with black paint. The over strokes used for shading are usually made with burnt umber or burnt sienna. The tray shown above is decorated with this freehand bronze technique.

Materials

Materials needed for this type of tin painting are the same as for country tin painting (page 2513), with a few exceptions (photograph 14). In tube oil paints, you will need only burnt umber or burnt sienna. Additional requirements are: one 18-by-29-inch piece of cotton velvet (for a palette); ½ pint black seal or ½ pint black oil-base enamel paint; a three- or four-pronged etching tool; and bronze powders (there are many colors available within the bronze category, but for this project, you will need one—gold).

Painting

As with country tin painting, practice this technique on frosted acetate before you decorate any tinware. Prepare the tin surface (Craftnotes, page 2512). While the background paint is drying, practice the design on acetate, following these directions. When you feel confident, transfer the design to the tin, using the magnesia method (page 2517). Complete the design on the tin, using the procedures that you practiced. Then finish the tin (Craftnotes, page 2512).

In doing freehand bronze work, use bronze powders. These come in plastic vials, but you do not use the powders directly from the containers. Instead, you need a palette made of cotton velvet, the only material that will hold the powders in place. At one time palettes were made of silk velvet, a fabric that is costly today. Velvets made of rayon or other synthetics, though they appear silky, are poor substitutes. The best choice is a cotton upholstery velvet with a very short pile. You may be able to buy a remnant at an upholstering shop.

To make the velvet palette, fold a piece of velvet approximately 18 by 20 inches square (Figure H). Bind the raw edges together to keep them from raveling; then continue folding (Figure I).

Now unfold the palette. Dip the tip of the palette knife into the vial of gold powder and place the powder carefully on one corner of the palette (Figure J), reserving the center and the right corner for other future colors. To serve as applicators, cut some 4-inch squares of the remaining velvet. Run an overcast stitch around the edges to keep bits of cloth from getting into the work.

The design shown on a tray can be used on any metal article. To make a basic tracing of the designs (without the etched black lines or shading over strokes), enlarge the patterns (Figure K) on tracing paper. Then go over the lines of the design with a crow-quill pen and ink. Place this pattern on cardboard and tape acetate over it, frosted side up, so you are ready to practice painting.

Black seal is the best paint to use for this work, but black enamel is a good second choice because it also dries quickly. Whichever you use, be sure it has an oil base. Stir the paint thoroughly. Then place a little in a bottle cap. Close the can tightly and store it upside down.

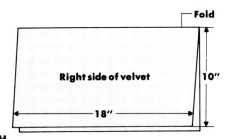

H
Figure H: To make a velvet palette for holding bronze powders of various colors, fold an 18-by-20-inch piece of velvet in half, right side out. Then bind the three raw edges with seam binding, using a hand- or machine-made stitch.

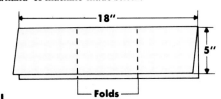

I
Figure I: Fold the velvet palette in half again to form a 5-by-18-inch rectangle. Then fold it in thirds, first bringing the left side to the right, and then the right side to the left. This is how the palette will be folded when not in use to keep three kinds of bronze powders in separate areas.

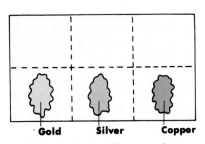

J
Figure J: For the freehand bronze project described here, you need only gold powder. Apply some to the lower left-hand corner of the palette, thus leaving space for other powders you may use later. The upper half of the palette will pick up some of the powder when the palette is folded.

K   1 square = ¼ inch

Figure K: To make patterns for the freehand bronze design pictured opposite, enlarge these designs on paper that you have ruled in ¼-inch squares. Copy the designs, one square at a time, transferring the lines from the small grid above to the larger grid you have made. These are the basic designs, without any etched lines or over strokes.

15: To get a tacky surface to which gold powder will adhere, brush black seal or black enamel within the outlines of the design. Begin in the center of the design and work out to the edges.

16: When the black paint has reached the right degree of tackiness—it snaps when you touch it but no black comes off on your finger—use a square of velvet to rub the gold powder onto it.

17: After applying the gold powder over the paint, use a stylus or a dry ball-point pen to scratch away the powder wherever you need to restore the black detail lines.

18: To make the fine lines that give a shaded effect, use a four-pronged etching tool. These lines may also be painted over the gold powder using a fine quill brush and black seal or enamel.

Using a square-tipped quill brush, fill the brush with black paint and try a few practice strokes on glass. When you are satisfied with the strokes, place a few on some part of the acetate away from the traced design. Then, every so often, you can return to this testing area to check the degree of tackiness reached by the paint. It will be at the proper stage when, as you touch it, it snaps back and no black comes away on your finger. Meanwhile, using the brushstrokes of country tin painting, cover the entire center design with black paint, working from the center out (photograph 15).

When the testing area is at the proper tackiness, the design area will soon be ready. Wrap a finger, either the index or middle finger, with one of the 4-inch velvet squares. Keep the velvet smooth over the ball of the finger, and hold the rest of the fabric with other fingers. Dip the ball of the finger into the gold powder on the palette. Then, with quick polishing motions, rub the gold onto the painted design. Keep the powder on the design as much as possible but don't worry about any outside the paint area. If necessary for coverage, go back over the design, adding more powder (photograph 16).

Sometimes the part painted first is ready for gold powder before the last is finished. Stop painting, apply gold powder as indicated, and continue painting.

When the painted areas have been covered with gold powder, you are ready either to etch or to paint in the black detail lines (top photograph, page 2520). To etch lines, use a stylus or dry ball-point pen to make all the black dividing lines on the flower, the outlines of each leaf, and the center veins on the leaves (photograph 17). The stylus will go through the gold, exposing the black beneath to give you the black lines you seek. If you pick up paint on the tip of the stylus, wipe it off before you proceed. Cross-hatching, as in the center of the flower, is done in the same manner. The very fine lines that give dimension to the flower and the leaves can be either etched or painted on. Any etching should be done at this time. Using a four-pronged etcher (photograph 18), place the prongs next to the center vein and draw the tool toward you. The gold will come away, leaving a shaded effect.

If you decide to paint in the shading lines, let the decorated article dry for 24 hours first. Then wash with mild soapy water, rinse, dry carefully, apply a coat of clear spar varnish, and allow 24 hours more for drying. When the varnish is dry, use a very fine quill brush and black seal or enamel to paint in the fine lines. Work from the center vein out to the edge on leaves and on flower petals. Let dry for 24 hours.

Now you are ready to apply the brown over strokes, following the photograph on page 2520. Put burnt umber or burnt sienna on the palette, and varnish in a bottle cap. Using a No. 2 or No. 3 square-tipped quill, fill the brush with varnish, then pick up some pigment on one side of the brush.

With the color side of the brush toward the center of the flower, paint a stroke around the center. Do the same all around the first and second layer of petals. Pick up more varnish and paint. With the color side of the brush toward the outside of the flower, make a stroke around the outside petals. Pick up more color and put a stroke over each leaf vein. Do the same around each flower in the center design on the border. Let dry for 24 hours; then finish the tray (Craftnotes, page 2512).

The antique stencil design on the top of a tin box, depicting a bowl of grapes, could be applied to any flat surface, although trays are most commonly decorated. As with all forms of stenciling, the most difficult step is the cutting of the stencils. Two colors of bronze lining powders—gold and copper—were used in this design.

Paint and Color
Antique stenciling on tin

$ 🎲 🧍 🎨

To reproduce antique stenciling on tinware, you will need most of the materials suggested for country tin painting (page 2513) plus a few additions, such as templates, as shown in photograph 19. For the tin-box design pictured above, you will need ½ yard of architect's linen, available at most art supply stores and the suppliers listed on page 2512. This finely woven, translucent fabric is coated with a sizing and will be cut with a razor blade to make the several stencils required. You will also need bronze lining powders in gold and copper; for other projects you may want to use silver or aluminum lining powders. These powders are similar to those used in doing freehand bronze painting (pages 2520 through 2522), but they are much finer. The hole punches pictured are a big help when a stencil design calls for small holes; a rubber dam punch (available at dental supply houses) has a revolving head that punches holes in five graduated sizes. No punches are needed for the antique stencil pictured, however. To practice antique stenciling, use black posterboard. Posterboard is very porous so it must be sealed before you can use it. Give it a coat of flat black oil-base paint or clear shellac. Set it aside to dry while you trace and cut your stencils.

19: Supplies needed for antique stenciling include (clockwise starting at the top): velvet palette; squares of velvet for applying the bronze powders; circle template; single-edged razor blades; India ink and crow-quill pen; French-curve template; assorted hole punches; and architect's linen.

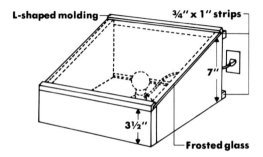

L-shaped molding — ¾" x 1" strips —
7"
3½"
Frosted glass

Making a light box

To make stencil cutting easier, make the light box diagramed above. Use ¾-inch pine for the sides, front, and bottom. Leave the back open for ventilation, but nail ¾-by-1-inch strips across the top and bottom edges of the back for rigidity. For the cutting surface, use a 12-inch-square of frosted glass (available at a glazier). Nail L-shaped molding where the top and bottom edges of the glass will be, so you can slide the glass in from the side. As the source of illumination, use a 15-watt light bulb. Attach electric cord to a porcelain receptacle (available at hardware stores); then place the receptacle in the light box and insert the bulb.

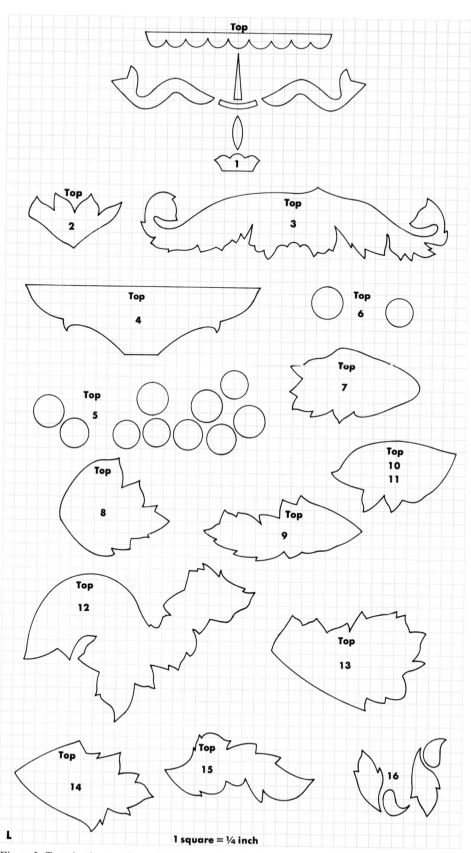

Figure L: To make the stencils needed for the antique design shown on page 2523, enlarge these patterns on tracing paper that you have ruled in ¼-inch squares. Copy the designs, one square at a time, transferring the lines from the small grid above to the larger grid that you have drawn. Then trace the enlarged stencil designs on pieces of architect's linen to make the stencils.

Drawing the Stencil

For this type of stenciling, you will draw and cut several small stencils, then use them one after the other in sequence to build up the design. For the design shown you need to enlarge the 16 separate stencils shown in Figure L.

The light box described opposite is useful in making stencils. I use opal glass, but frosted glass or even clear window glass will work. If you buy clear glass, tape tracing paper under it so you don't have to stare at the lighted bulb below.

For each stencil, cut a piece of architect's linen large enough to allow a 1½-to-2-inch margin of linen around the design. Place a piece of translucent linen, dull side up, on the light box glass with enlarged stencil No. 1 underneath. Secure it with masking tape. Turn on the light, and with crow-quill pen and India ink, copy the design onto the linen. If the pen point is not making a clear line, wet it with warm water or dip it in household ammonia, wipe it dry, and try again. You can use templates or such tools as a French curve or triangles to help you draw accurately. After you draw the first stencil, mark it No. 1, put it in a heavy plastic bag, waxed-paper sandwich bag, or file folder, and keep it flat. Cut another piece of linen and trace shape No. 2. Continue cutting the pieces of linen, tracing the shapes, numbering the stencils, and placing them in a plastic bag. Draw all the grapes shown in stencils No. 5 and 6 on a single piece of linen, allowing 1½ inches between each group and 1½ inches along the edges.

Cutting the Stencil

Cutting a stencil calls for great care and patience. Every error will show. Avoid pressing on the razor blade as you cut. Never cut a second hole until the first is perfect. Work slowly. Using a light box, follow this procedure: lay the linen for the first stencil to be cut on the glass of the box. The point of the razor will slice through the linen easily. Do not press so hard that you scratch the glass. Move the linen slowly with one hand as you cut with the other hand. At sharp points in the design, insert the point of the blade and draw it toward you, moving the linen with your free hand. Watch where you are going, not where you've been. At curves, be sure you do cut curves, not angles. If you leave any angles, go back and shave them off. Change blades whenever one begins to drag. Correct each opening as you go. If you slip and cut too far, place a piece of transparent tape over the mistake, on the dull side of the linen; then recut if necessary. Continue in this manner until the entire stencil is cut. Hold it up to the light. Study the holes, not the surrounding linen, looking for any flaws, ragged edges, or angles. If the stencil still needs work, it is better to cut it slightly larger and have it perfect than to leave it the original size but imperfect.

When you cut a leaf stencil (photograph 20), start at the point of a lobe and curve down and into the center of the opening, cutting out a bit at a time.

To cut grapes, insert the point of the blade anywhere along the marked line of one of the grapes. Turn the linen continually with one hand, keeping an eye on the blade's progress, until you have cut out the entire circle. No one can cut a round grape perfectly on the first attempt: it takes practice. Check the stencil for angles and rough edges, and round them off.

Stenciling

Once you have cut all the stencils for the design, the rest is easy. Make a velvet palette and place the lining powders on it (Figures H, I, and J, page 2521). (Do not use the same palette that you use with coarser powders for freehand bronze work.) On the practice posterboard, use a silver pencil to mark the area you will stencil. If your project is a tray, for example, lay the tray on the posterboard upside down and draw around it. Then, again using the silver pencil, draw guidelines for the border stripes, but do not paint them at this point.

Varnish the entire posterboard with clear, high-gloss spar varnish (not the quick-drying type). Flow it on lightly with a natural-bristle brush, making sure the entire area is covered. Drying takes five hours or longer (high humidity will slow the drying). The varnish must reach the stage of tackiness where it will snap when you touch it, but not leave a finger print. When you think it is ready, test outside the outlined area of the posterboard by laying the linen leaf stencil on the varnish, shiny side down. If it doesn't stick, the varnish is ready.

20: To cut a stencil, lay it on a piece of window glass and apply gentle pressure on the back of a single-edged razor blade. These lobed leaves are cut in sections, with each cut ending near the center of the leaf. A well-cut stencil has sharp, crisp details.

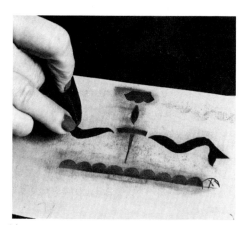

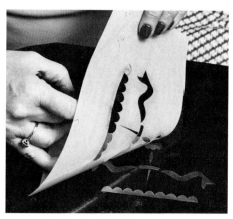

21: Place the first stencil on the tacky surface of partly dry varnish. Then rub gold-colored lining powder into the cutout areas until they are solidly filled in. Carry and apply the powder with a square of velvet wrapped around a finger.

22: After rubbing on the powder, lift the stencil carefully and check to make sure your application technique is leaving a perfect impression. Set aside the stencil to be cleaned later with paint thinner before using it again.

23: Place the second stencil in the center of the first impression and apply gold-colored powder to within ½ to ¼ inch of where the first stencil shows in the opening; as the color fades off it will give a three-dimensional effect.

To give you the feel of stenciling, make an impression with the leaf stencil. An impression results when bronze powder is used to fill the entire cutout area, rather than shading from light to dark. Wrap your index or middle finger with a small square of velvet. Keep the velvet smooth over the ball of the finger, holding the surplus velvet with your other fingers. Touch the velvet-covered finger to the powder. Wipe excess powder onto the back of the other hand or tap it off onto a clean section of the palette. Use very little powder: it goes a long way. You can always add more, but an excess is difficult to get rid of once applied. With a new piece of velvet, you should barely be able to see the powder you are using. Hold the leaf stencil gently in place. Using a circular finger-painting motion, polish the powder into the stencil opening, working from the outside edges in to the center. Always work from the outside in; otherwise the powder will work under the stencil. Polish until no excess powder shows. Gently lift the stencil and examine your handwork. If the powder is beyond the points of the leaf, either you used too much or you worked from the center toward the edges. If powder has been deposited in a straight line beyond the outer edge of the stencil, you did not leave enough margin or your circular polishing motion was too large. Keep practicing on edges of the posterboard until you can achieve a perfect impression with each of the stencils.

Clean each stencil with turpentine or paint thinner and let it dry. Next, practice the design within the outlined area of the posterboard. Read all the instructions through before you begin. If you work slowly, your varnish may get too dry before you finish. When this happens, let the posterboard (or the tin piece, in later stages) dry for 24 hours. Wash the stenciled surface with warm, soapy water, rinse, dry, revarnish, wait until the varnish is tacky, then begin exactly where you left off. If you are careful the varnish will not damage what you have already stenciled. Before you are finished, you will apply many coats of varnish over the stenciled work.

Stencil No. 1 (page 2524) is the bowl top with the centerpiece and the streamers. This is the key piece of the entire design. Place the bottom of the bowl top across the center of the outlined area. Pick up some gold-colored lining powder on a velvet square and wipe off the excess. Polish from the outside in, filling the cutout area entirely with gold. Be sure all areas are covered (photographs 21 and 22).

All the rest of the pieces will be shaded except the large group of grapes. Place stencil No. 2 in the center, just over the needle-shaped section of stencil No. 1, with two of the points on each side of the bowl. Pick up the gold powder, wipe off any excess, and polish from the outside of the points to the center. But this time, polish only to within ½ to ¼ inch of the already stenciled piece (photograph 23). The powder will ride farther than you expect; so be careful. This shading will make the pointed section look as though it's behind what has already been stenciled. To keep from going too far when you are shading, you can place a fingertip or a piece of linen over the already stenciled area. But don't press hard; this is merely a guide so you won't stencil too close to the preceding stencil.

24: The second, third, and fourth stencils have been applied to the design. Note how these last three stencils shade away toward the vertical center elements.

25: The fifth stencil, consisting of ten grape shapes, has been applied on top of the bowl. The ability to cut grape stencils well will come only with practice.

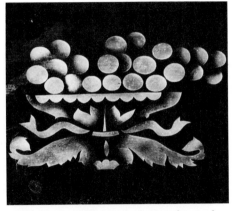

26: Use the two different-sized grape shapes of the sixth stencil over and over again, shading away near the grape already in place, until the bowl is filled to overflowing.

Place No. 3, the bowl bottom, on the board and apply gold powder as you did with No. 2. This bowl bottom is shaded up to the sections already stenciled. Stencil No. 4 is the under bowl; it is done in gold-colored lining powder and is shaded in under the bowl top and under the leaves. It requires just a bit of polishing at the edges. Avoid touching any of the pieces already placed; shade away to nothing (photograph 24).

The group of grapes, stencil No. 5, is placed on top of the bowl and polished in solidly with gold powder (photograph 25).

Stencil No. 6 includes two separate grapes. Use it repeatedly to the left, right, and top center to fill out the grape cluster, shading each grape as illustrated (photograph 26).

Leaf stencil No. 7 is placed to the left side of the bowl. This and all other leaves should be stenciled in copper-colored lining powder rather than gold. Begin polishing from the outside and shade as you approach the bowl and grapes, leaving a dark area. Leaf No. 8 is placed on the right side of the bowl below the grapes and is also shaded.

Copper-colored leaf No. 9 is placed above the left leaf, and on the left side of the bowl. Shade and polish, leaving dark areas around the grapes and the previous leaf.

Leaf No. 10 is on the left side of the bowl between the two previous leaves. Shade and polish. No. 11 is the point of the leaf you see between the two end grapes on the right side of the bowl. It is made by reusing the point of leaf No. 10. Shade it in behind the grapes.

Leaf No. 12 covers a large area on the left side of the bowl giving the effect of several leaves. It is shaded in behind all three previously placed leaves and nearly meets the bottom of the bowl. Leaf No. 13 is placed on the far right side of the bowl beyond the grapes and other leaves and is shaded. No. 14 is placed beyond No. 13 on the right side and shaded. No. 15 is shaded against the bottom right side of the bowl. Use leaf No. 7 and shade it in several times behind the grapes and other leaves at the top of the bowl to round out the design (photograph 27).

27: With the addition of copper-colored leaves, the center design has been completely stenciled. If the shape of the area seems to need a fuller design, you can add more leaves to fill any empty spaces.

When stenciling is completed, wait 24 hours, then wash the stenciled surface with warm water and soap. Rinse and gently pat dry. The process will not remove any of the stencil. Varnish the entire surface that you have stenciled and let it dry for 24 hours. Then paint the stripes on the posterboard, following the directions given on page 2517, and photographs 11 and 12.

All the leaf veins in this design are made with black brushstrokes. Use black seal or black enamel and a square-tipped quill brush, painting all the veins shown in the color photograph on page 2523. Allow 24 hours for drying, and varnish the surface again.

This completes the practice design. If you are satisfied with your work, follow the same procedures to stencil the design on metal. When you do the actual project, however, complete the finishing procedure described in the Craftnotes, page 2512.

For related entries, see "Folk Art," "Rosemaling," and "Stenciling."

TOPIARY

Living Sculpture

Topiary is the art of training and pruning living plants so they simulate sculptures. It was practiced extensively in the formal gardens of royal palaces and country estates. By selectively pruning yews, boxwood, hemlock, privet, and ivy, topiary gardeners were able to develop fantastic geometrical and animal figures. These often took 20 years or more to create. Entire menageries of animals, some amusing, others frightening, were designed primarily for the entertainment of guests. In addition, mazelike hedgerows were laid out in geometrical patterns. At the end of their labyrinthine passages, there was often a statue, a fountain, or a tranquil pool.

The art of topiary is little practiced today except at historic restorations and commercial parks. But certain forms of this nearly lost art require little skill or time to execute. On a small scale—with or without the aid of supporting structures—topiary can be revived in gardens large or small, even with indoor plants. The neatly clipped hedges of yesterday's formal landscapes—their tops flattened, rounded, or trimmed at intervals into geometric figures—lend themselves to more modest home gardens if the scale is suitably reduced.

Topiary's reputation fluctuates depending on the style favored at any one time. Those who subscribe to the classic school of landscaping, a formal, geometric style, tend to like topiary forms; those who favor the romantic school, an informal, naturalistic style, tend to avoid them. But since so many homes include something of both worlds, topiary is rarely completely out of character. For many plants to thrive without sprawling, their growth must be restrained in any event. Anyone who regularly clips a hedge or trains a vine can let this practical necessity serve an aesthetic end as well using topiary techniques.

James Huntley is a landscape architect who works primarily with privately owned gardens. But he has also designed many public gardens, including those at the General Motors Exhibit of the New York World's Fair, the airports at Columbia and Greenville-Spartanburg in South Carolina, and the Nassau County Research Library in Hempstead, New York. His office is in Southampton, Long Island.

Opposite: A brace of sculpted topiary swans seems to float on a sea of privet hedge. To make such elaborate compositions takes years of patient pruning. Working on a smaller scale, you can train some plants into ornamental shapes in only a few months.

Left: A topiary poodle frolics atop an evergreen at the entrance to a formal garden. The geometrical shapes beside the hedge opening in the background are also topiary.

A topiary showpiece like this doesn't require a baronial manor for a background. It can be created quickly for den or living room by training fast-growing ivy over a form of wood and wire.

Few gardeners today have either the time or the patience to train slow-growing plant varieties into fancy shapes. But it is possible to work with fast-growing plants, such as privet and ivy, to produce unique living sculptures that add interest to the most prosaic garden. To do so, the gardener must know when to be aggressive with his pruning shears and when to exercise restraint. If a little pruning is good, it doesn't follow that a lot is better. Successful topiary work depends on coordination of eye and hand, imagination, and knowledge of the growing habits of plants.

Greenery and Growing Things
Simple geometrical topiary

For your first topiary project, try your hand at shaping ivy into a cube shape. This kind of green sculpture makes an interesting indoor adornment for any area where you might place an ordinary potted plant—a coffee table, window sill, or entrance foyer, for example. English ivy (*Hedera helix*) is one of the most adaptable of ornamental indoor vines. It will flourish if it gets several hours of sunlight a day, but it can also be grown in indirect reflected light. Choose a small-leafed variety such as needlepoint ivy. It has a neater appearance when shaped than the large-leafed varieties. By letting it grow on a shaped form, you can create almost any topiary figure you can imagine, indoors or out. Fabricated forms are sold in garden-supply stores, but you can make less expensive forms with exterior plywood covered with chicken wire or scraps of aluminum window screening. As long as the ivy is well rooted in good potting soil and is kept fed and watered, the vines will continue to grow. They will require periodic grooming if you want to retain the cube shape. This involves tying, clipping, and occasionally redirecting wayward vines.

To make the topiary cube pictured at left, you will need—in addition to a dozen or more healthy ivy plants—an 8-by-20-inch piece of ½-inch exterior-grade plywood; a 6-inch square of ¾-inch exterior grade plywood; three 24-inch lengths of L-shaped shelf-bracket strips of rustproof aluminum (available at hardware stores); a dozen ½-inch wood screws; small staples (which can be driven either with a staple gun or a hammer); 1 yard of 4-foot-high chicken wire; a can of dark-green spray paint; a planting pot 12 to 16 inches in diameter with provision for drainage; sufficient potting soil to fill the pot; and a few yards of florist's wire, or freezer-bag ties. Household tools are all that are needed, although a saber saw is recommended for cutting the plywood.

The Support Form
Although a topiary project takes months to complete, the support form is easy to make. Cut the ½-inch plywood in half to make two 8-by-10-inch rectangles. Draw rounded corners with a pencil and string; then cut them out with a saber saw or coping saw. Then cut a ½-inch-wide slot from the edge to the center on the longest side of each rectangle. Sand all the edges smooth. Slide the two rectangles together into the slots to form a cross-lapped shape (photograph 1). Screw the aluminum shelf-bracket strips to this frame (photograph 2). Align them so they bridge the interior angles on three sides—the fourth will need no support—and set the ends flush with the top edge of the plywood form. To make a base for the structure, use a vise or heavy pliers to bend the bottom ends of the bracket strips outward at right angles, 3 inches from the bottom. Screw these feet to the center of the 6-inch square of ¾-inch plywood. Use at least two screws wherever you fasten a bracket strip to wood (screws can go through slots as well as screwholes).

Shaping the Wire Armature
Wrap the chicken wire several times around the plywood frame. Use pliers to bend and shape the overlapping ends to achieve a cube form on the frame. Wear gloves—the cut ends of wire are sharp. If you need to cut the wire in places, use tin snips. Twist cut ends around uncut wires with the pliers. When the armature has acquired a neat and compact shape, staple the wire to the plywood edges. Then spray the entire form—plywood, brackets, and chicken wire—with dark-green paint (photograph 3). This will help camouflage it until the ivy hides it completely, and

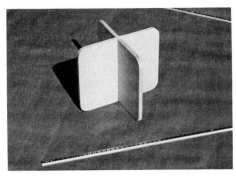

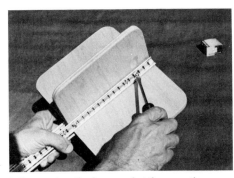

1: To make a simple, cube-shaped topiary frame, assemble two notched squares of exterior-grade plywood into a cross-shaped form with rounded corners. Use a saber saw or jigsaw to make these cuts with ease.

2: Strengthen the form, and at the same time make a post for it to stand on, by attaching aluminum shelf-bracket strips. Drive two screws through holes in the brackets into the wood, so the metal strip bridges the joint at an angle.

3: Wrap chicken wire around the frame to form a cube-shaped armature for the ivy to cling to. Then spray the entire structure a dark-green color to improve its appearance and to keep the chicken wire from rusting.

4: Initially, you can fasten the ivy strands to the chicken wire with florist's tape or freezer-bag ties, but don't twist them tightly. As the ivy grows it will attach itself to the wire.

5: Train new growth onto the chicken wire. Once the foliage cube has filled out to your satisfaction, hiding the support structure, trim off leaves that reach outside the desired shape.

will protect the chicken wire from rust. When the paint is dry, set the form into a large planter. It should have a drainage hole and saucer, or a layer of gravel at the bottom. You can adjust the height of the armature by putting a layer of gravel beneath the plywood base. Add potting soil above the base until the planter is about two-thirds full.

Training the Vines

Set the rooted ivy plants in the pot and pack them in firmly with soil. Water the plants (do not fertilize until the plants are established); then let them rest for a day or so before starting to train the vines. Take each vine up close to the support post and around the wire cube, tying it at frequent intervals with florist's wire or green freezer-bag ties (photograph 4). Twist these ties loosely so they do not cut into the vine as it grows. In time the ivy will send out tendrils that will attach it to the wire; then the ties may be removed. Avoid twisting or looping the vines and be careful not to break them.

It's better not to try to create instant topiary by covering too much of the frame at the beginning. Wait for the plants to grow so they can fill out the frame naturally. With regular grooming to remove wayward strands, the topiary will develop a neat and compact appearance. Each day, if possible, snip off any dead leaves (photograph 5), and spray the leaves with a fine mist. About once a week, tie new growth to the frame to hide exposed stems and the frame itself. Cleaning the leaves with cotton swabs dipped in soapy water will keep the ivy looking bright and fresh.

The entrance patio of a Victorian house is an appropriate place to display a topiary form. Here, three ivy balls conceal the frame of wood and wire to which they cling.

Greenery and Growing Things
A three-ball ivy topiary

Using the armature construction and plant training methods described in the preceding project, you can move on to larger projects designed for outdoor display. The same tools and materials can be used to make elaborate geometrical forms or whimsical animal shapes. For example, the triple topiary balls that sometimes crown estate hedges of boxwood or privet can be simulated with fast-growing ivy to give you dramatic plants for an entrance porch or patio, as pictured at left.

To make the balls, you need: a 2-foot square of ½-inch exterior-grade plywood; an 8-inch square of ¾-inch exterior-grade plywood; one 24-inch length and two 48-inch lengths of aluminum shelf-bracket strips; 2 yards of 4-foot-high chicken wire; three dozen ½-inch wood screws; and at least a dozen needlepoint-ivy plants.

Using a pencil and string draw two 10-inch circles, two 8-inch circles, and two 6-inch circles on the 2-foot square of plywood. Cut out the circles with a saber saw or coping saw. In each circle, cut a ½-inch-wide slot from the edge to the center, and sand the edges smooth. Cut out an 8-inch circle from the ¾-inch plywood for the base. Fit the circle pairs together to form cross frames for spheres (photograph 6). Set the frames on a worktable spacing them 4 inches apart. Attach a 48-inch bracket strip to all three frames, the top of the strip flush with the top of the smallest frame (photograph 7). Use two screws in each frame. Attach the other 48-inch bracket strip to the opposite side of the frames. Then fasten the 24-inch bracket to the largest frame only, the top of the bracket flush with the top of the frame.

With a vise or pliers, bend the bottom of the three bracket strips outward at right angles (photograph 8), and screw them into the plywood base (photograph 9).

Using tin snips or cutting pliers, cut 30-inch, 24-inch, and 18-inch squares of chicken wire. Fit each one over and around the corresponding frame, in order of size. Staple the wire to the plywood edges, bending, shaping, and cutting as necessary so the wire forms a ball of at least double thickness all around the form. Bend all cut ends to the inside of the ball. Set the form into a planter at least 24 inches in diameter; then plant and train the ivy as detailed on page 2531.

6: To make a three-ball topiary form, first assemble three notched plywood disks to make ball-shaped frames. Slots to the center of each pair of disks let you slide them together.

7: Hold the three wooden forms together with three aluminum shelf-bracket strips, spacing the forms 4 inches apart and arranging them in a tree shape with the smallest ball on top.

8: Bend the lower 4 inches of each shelf-bracket strip to form a right angle, using a vise or heavy pliers. For stability, be sure to make the bend at the same point on all strips.

9: Screw the feet at the bottoms of the strips onto the circular base that goes into the planter. If necessary for fit, cut off projecting ends with tin snips or a hacksaw.

Greenery and Growing Things
Shaping a privet hedge

Traditional topiary is not as simple to do as training ivy vines to climb on a wire form. Such plant sculptures are usually found only on large estates because they are expensive in plant materials and labor. Commercially made metal armatures for large forms are costly. But with patience, good results can be achieved with less valuable plants, using homemade armatures or no supports at all. The globe atop a neatly trimmed privet hedge, shown at right, required no frame at all. The yew dog, page 2529, has a simple homemade frame. But the privet swans, page 2528 were shaped with commercial armatures.

You might like to try making topiary sculptures from existing hedges or shrubs. If you have plants that have become so bulky they are beginning to dominate the landscape, they should be pruned in any case. This gives you an opportunity to begin work on a geometrical animal or shape.

Topiary pruning begins with cutting out all dead branches and thinning out the old growth, especially in the center of the plant. This lets more light penetrate the center of the plant, encouraging compact new growth at that point. Once this basic pruning is done, stand back and study the plant to see what shape it naturally suggests. Picture the main branches as a sort of skeleton and the mass of foliage, present or to come, as the flesh of the form. Visualize where extremities could be expected to grow in the future. Note strong young shoots that eventually could form arms, heads, tails, or other appendages if neighboring growth were cut back. Keep in mind, too, what shapes would be appropriate in the landscape. Not everyone would appreciate an elephant topiary in the neighborhood.

In shaping shrub-sized evergreens, the simplest form to attempt is a sphere. Hatfield yews and common boxwood have a naturally rounded shape and need only light trimming. This globe crowning a privet hedge required more work but no internal supporting structure.

Geometrical topiary forms like these tiered and crowned privet cubes have been classics in formal gardens for centuries. Since no two plants ever grow exactly alike, creating landscapes of such perfect symmetry requires much patience and skill.

More amusing than beautiful, a full-sized topiary elephant made of four separate juniper shrubs stands in a flower patch at the Walt Disney World in Florida. A complex hidden armature is indispensable in creating such a living sculpture.

The sweeping lines of a sculpted privet hedge frame a croquet court on a Long Island estate. Guidelines of taut string helped the gardener to prune the perfectly straight top.

At the Nursery

If you shop for plants to sculpt, buy young ones so you can train them gradually as they fill in. The best varieties are boxwood, yew, hemlock, and privet. (The narrow-leaved evergreens—yew and hemlock—are more resistant to winter damage in the north than the broad-leaved evergreens, boxwood and privet.) Boxwood is slow-growing, compact, and easy to train; it does best in areas without extremes of winter cold or summer heat. Boxwood does best in full sun or light shade. It requires moist soil and should be planted or transplanted in the spring. Soon after planting, mulch the bed with a 1-inch layer of peat moss or wood chips. For the first year, spray the foliage with a fine mist during hot spells.

Yew is hardier and has a beautiful feathery texture and a dark-green color. Like boxwood, it tends to be rather expensive, but it requires little care, flourishing in bright sun or shade. It does best in well-drained, slightly acid soil. Fertilize it in spring with a light application of cottonseed meal, then water it well.

Hemlock, though coarser and not as manageable, is more economical than boxwood or yew because it grows faster. It thrives in cool, moist conditions and almost any light level, though in a warm climate it favors shade. Fertilizer is usually unnecessary, but if new growth seems sparse or pale, apply a light layer of cottonseed meal in early spring.

Privet is inexpensive, fast-growing, and easily shaped in regions warm enough for it to survive the winter, but it has a less pleasing texture than the others. It does well in sun or shade, in any soil, and is tolerant of drought. Fertilizer is generally unnecessary and should be applied only if growth seems unnaturally slow.

The First Shaping

Once you have chosen a plant and have groomed it (in the case of an old plant) or planted it (a new one), you are ready to begin shaping. (A topiary design can be made with a single plant, several plants in a tableau arrangement, or several plants combined into a single sculpture.)

Do not attempt to complete a finished form in one pruning operation. Finished results in hedge topiary, unlike ivy topiary, are achieved in years (perhaps four or five) rather than in weeks. If the plant is healthy and has not been recently pruned, the first pruning can be on the severe side, cutting back to well within the finished shape that is visualized. You should let the plant grow into the form you want so the

Bibliography
Art of Shaping Shrubs, Trees, and Other Plants by Tatsuo and Kiyoko Ishimoto, Crown Publishers, Inc.

The Book of Topiary by Charles H. Curtis, John Lane.

Espaliers and Vines for the Home Gardener by Harold O. Perkins, Van Nostrand Reinhold Company.

Evergreens by James Underwood Crockett, Time-Life Books.

Hedges, Screens, and Windbreaks by Donald Wyman, Whittlesey House.

Pruning Handbook, edited by Paul F. Frese, Brooklyn Botanic Garden.

Topiary and Ornamental Hedges by Miles Hadfield, St. Martin's Press, Inc.

Trained and Sculptured Plants, edited by Emily L. Brown, Brooklyn Botanic Garden.

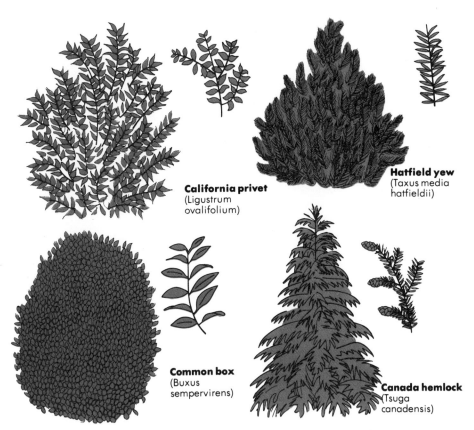

California privet
(Ligustrum ovalifolium)

Hatfield yew
(Taxus media hatfieldii)

Common box
(Buxus sempervirens)

Canada hemlock
(Tsuga canadensis)

These four plants are the ones most commonly used in topiary. Their overall shape and size, leaf structure, and resilience make them well suited to hedge-shear artistry.

surface will be evenly covered with foliage. Heavy pruning will leave you with a rather sorry-looking plant for several weeks, but the varieties mentioned are generally quite resilient. As new side shoots grow through a period of several weeks, tie, twist, and prune them to the shape you seek. Prune boxwood in the early spring, before new growth has started. For yew, hemlock, or privet, wait until midsummer. Never prune evergreen plants near the end of a growing season; pruning stimulates tender new growth that will be damaged by cold weather.

Simple topiary forms require no internal support. Plants like Hatfield yew and common boxwood that naturally grow into rounded shapes can be turned into perfect globes with no more than careful pruning. A globe may also be squared off, layered into tiers, or trimmed into a spiral, if you remember that parts of the plant constantly shaded by other parts may lose their foliage.

The more elaborate your design becomes, the more likely you are to need a mechanical skeleton. Commercial armatures can cost $1,000 or more. But you can assemble smaller supports of ¼-inch soft steel rods, available from building-supply houses. Bend the rod to the shape you seek using pipe wrenches, drive it into the ground inside the plant, and tie the branches to it with rawhide strips, available at shoe-repair shops.

Make any such armature larger than the plant now is. As the plant matures, new growth can be tied to the outer reaches of the armature. Each year, prune the plant heavily at the same time as you did the original shaping to guide its growth and maintain a clean outline. You can also do light trimming four or more times each summer for a neat appearance. (But avoid trimming boxwood in hot weather.) To accelerate new growth, you can root-prune the evergreens listed above in early spring by driving a spade into the soil in a circular pattern about one foot from the trunk.

For related projects and crafts, see "Bonsai," "Organic Gardening," and "Yard Environments."

Espalier

A plant-training technique closely linked to topiary is espalier, the art of making trees or shrubs grow flat against a building wall, railing, trellis, or other support. For this purpose, only the healthiest of young plants are selected, because the training process is taxing—though it must be constructive, since fruit trees that have undergone skillful espalier treatment are notably fine producers of fruit.

Some nurseries sell young fruit trees, dogwood, fire thorn, and other varieties, already partially trained to a predetermined form. The most common espalier shapes are shown opposite. Living examples of two types are pictured at right (random espalier) and below (standard espalier). To produce these shapes, branches are tied to a frame or onto anchors driven in a wall. They are controlled, little by little, year after year. The tying techniques may be essentially the same as those used in topiary (page 2535), or the ties may be made with strips of lead fastened to the frame or wall.

Espaliered plants must be severely pruned in early spring, before growth starts; then they are lightly trimmed once each month during the growing season. In the first pruning of a main trunk, the prior year's new growth is cut back to half its length. When the tree has reached maturity, only one bud per year is allowed to grow. Side shoots are generally.cut to about 4 inches in spring, and are repeatedly trimmed in summer to prevent branches from forming where they are not wanted. Fruit and foliage is constantly thinned. The crown, especially, must be kept sparse, so lower branches receive abundant sunlight. Diseased, broken, or dead branches are removed whenever they are noticed. Cuts larger than 1½ inches in diameter are sealed with pruning paint.

An espaliered dogwood blossoms in profusion against a brick wall at the reception center of Philipsburg Manor, a seventeenth-century Dutch restoration in Tarrytown, New York. The branches are tied to almost invisible wires and have been trained to grow in this shape over a long period of time.

An ancient espaliered pear tree, its bare lower branches clearly showing the lines of its former training, still bears fruit on its upper branches.

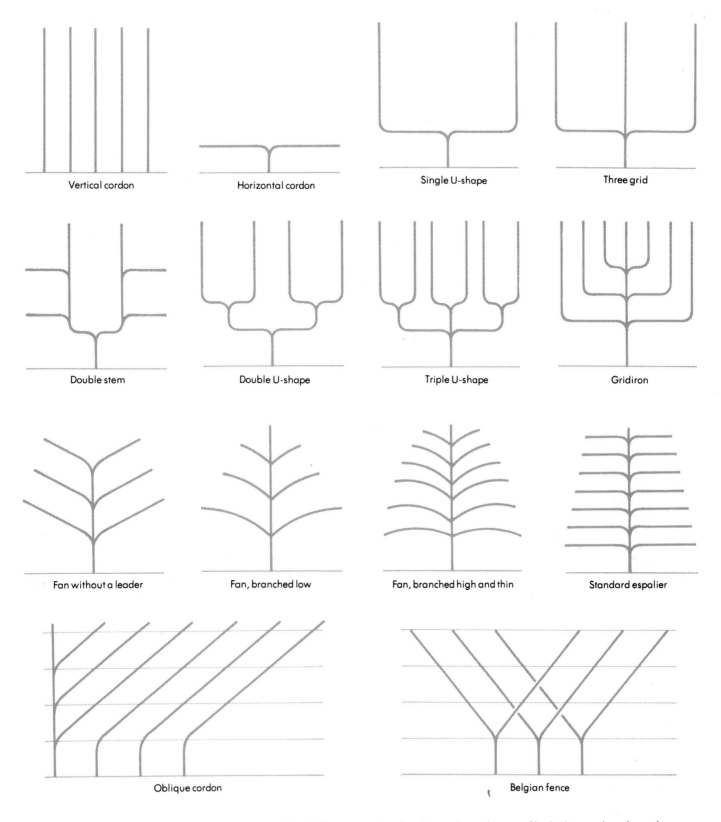

Vertical cordon

Horizontal cordon

Single U-shape

Three grid

Double stem

Double U-shape

Triple U-shape

Gridiron

Fan without a leader

Fan, branched low

Fan, branched high and thin

Standard espalier

Oblique cordon

Belgian fence

The frames the plants grow on generally consist of a grid work of lattice strips or wires spaced 12 to 16 inches apart, or a series of posts at wider intervals. The less visible the supports are, the greater the impact. The flowering dogwood shown at right seems to cling to the brick wall like a vine.

Espalier demands much more of both plant and gardener than topiary. Good results require design training, plant knowledge, and perseverance. There are many subtle points to be mastered. A wealth of techniques, passed from generation to generation, gives espalier a distinguished place among the gardening arts.

TOTEM POLES
Symbols of Family Pride

The Indians of the Pacific Northwest who originated the towering wooden columns called totem poles were trained for the job from childhood. Only a few of the candidates achieved the rank of master carver.

But if you are willing to settle for being less demanding than the wealthy Indian chiefs who commissioned the original totem poles, you do not need special skill to do an interesting job of carving and painting a totem pole to decorate your own garden. The carving done by the Indian craftsmen in the original totem poles was not deep; cuts rarely exceeded an inch in depth, even in a pole a foot in diameter. Nor does the carving need to be three-dimensional; Indian totems were rarely carved completely "in the round." In fact, if you create a primitive-looking image and decorate it with brilliantly colored paint, your pole may look quite authentic.

To do as the Indians did, choose totem figures that have some special meaning to you—perhaps a big fish you once caught, or a pet you remember fondly. If you plan to carve a pole that tells a story, as the Indian poles did, let it be read from top to bottom.

The First Totem Poles

Stretching from southeast Alaska to Washington's Puget Sound, North America's northwest coast is a region of extraordinary grandeur. The land is forested with red cedar, spruce, hemlock, cottonwood, and pine. Here dwelt—and dwell today—Indian nations with names such as Tlingit, Tsimsyan, Haida, Kwakiutl, Bella Coola, Nootka, Quilliute, Coast Salish. They developed the exceptional occupation of carving and painting totem poles.

Totems, the subjects depicted on the poles, were natural objects, usually animals, believed by the Indians to have special power. A totem was adopted by a tribe, a family, or an individual as a guardian spirit. Common totems were the eagle, fox, bear, wolf, beaver, whale, owl, frog, and raven. By the time the first European explorers arrived, the totem pole's greatest importance was as a memorial to the dead.

Towering Totem Poles

The custom of erecting very tall totem poles flourished only after the Indians obtained metal carving tools from Russian colonists in the eighteenth century. The poles that existed when the first white explorers arrived were only 10 or 15 feet tall, but later they rose as high as 81 feet. The oldest known poles were carved by the Haidas of Queen Charlotte Island about 300 years ago: these first poles were simply carvings on the pillars that supported beams of large wooden houses. Later, totem figures were carved on separate posts which were attached to the pillars. Finally, free-standing poles were erected in front of the houses.

One of the best examples surviving from the golden age of totem-pole carving (far left) stands today at the entrance to New York's Museum of the American Indian. It was made around 1875 at Kasaan Village, Prince of Wales Island, Alaska, for Chief Eagle of the Kaigani Haida tribe. More than 43 feet tall, it weighs 4,490 pounds. An eagle perches at the top. The blank area below it, indicating the chief's prestige, is followed by a grizzly bear, a second grizzly bear and his wife, a frog person, a beaver, and a hunter. Closeup views of the latter three images appear at bottom left, top right, and bottom right, opposite. It is often hard to identify a design because the artists distributed various parts of the animal body around the trunk, as in the case of the frog.

Whale

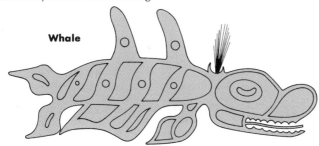

Lloyd Kennedy makes totem poles and studies dreams. Born in West Virginia and partly of Creek Indian ancestry, he has worked with Boy Scouts for most of his life and was a Scout master and camp counselor for more than ten years. He studied philosophy at West Virginia University and Columbia University, and teaches retarded children in Pomona, New York.

Salmon

Bear

Kinds of Totem Poles

In early times, when a man was about to carve a totem pole, he would fast to become humble so he could take his work seriously. But later poles became objects of prestige. Feuds erupted if someone dared erect a pole taller than his neighbor's, and carvers tried to outdo one another in crafting skill.

The purposes of the poles gradually changed. Some came to be mere coats-of-arms. Erected near the front door of a house, the pole sometimes had a hole in it through which visitors had to pass. Motifs boasted of the importance of the people who lived there. Other poles, erected in pairs, served as boundary markers. Still others were erected to shame debtors, to report a scandal, or to express ridicule, anger, or indignation. Such uses often led to fighting and even warfare.

Totem Pole Motifs

The symbols on an Indian totem pole summarized a story. The complete story, often a popular myth, was assumed to be known to all, and in any case it was recited at the pole-raising celebration. The poles were read narratively from top to bottom and, contrary to the expression "low man on the totem pole," the arrangement of the figures rarely indicated their importance.

The Craftsman

An Indian youth who showed a talent for carving was gradually initiated by a medicine man into the secret lore of his clan. He was also apprenticed to a master carver.

When a man, usually a chief, decided he was wealthy enough to afford a totem pole, he would enlist a good carver, and together they would select a suitable tree, often red cedar. The tree was felled, stripped of branches and bark, and towed by canoe to a secret carving place. There, apprentices did much of the rough shaping, but the final carving, as well as the painting, was left to the master carver. The paints, bright but quick to fade, were made from animal oils and blood, salmon eggs, charcoal, graphite, ocher, and moss. They were applied with brushes made of animal fur.

Today's Carvings

If you decide to try one of the projects described here, the tools and materials you need can be obtained at little cost. Indian carvers had only simple knives and chisels, so you do not need a very extensive workshop to make a totem figure. The carvings can be cut in any wood that is not too hard. If you want to try a pole, you might see if you can get a section of an old pole from the telephone company. I don't recommend that you attempt to carve a pole more than 10 feet long. A pole taller than that is heavy and difficult to maneuver. If you have a dead tree that is still standing, you can strip it of branches and bark and carve it in place, working from a ladder to whatever height you think is safe. (Have a professional cut off the upper trunk and branches before you start.) Safest of all is to carve and paint the pole on the ground, then erect the finished work.

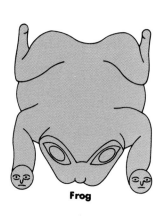

Frog

Thunderbird

Low-relief mask motifs come from all over the world. This wall plaque is modeled on a ceremonial mask from New Guinea. Whittled from a pine board and stained black, its hollowed eyes and grooved headdress are accented with white paint.

A wall plaque in the form of a totem mask provides a good introduction to totem-pole carving. The low-relief carving in the mask is done in the same style as most pole carving. The custom of carving totem poles is believed to be an extension of primitive mask making.

Carving and Molding
A totem-mask wall plaque

Many people, once they decide to make a totem pole, simply round up the tools and materials and do it. In carving rough, large-scale wood sculptures, interesting results are not difficult to achieve. There is a great deal of leeway for individual style; so in the end, anything goes.

But in my experience in teaching young campers to make totem figures, I have found two preliminary exercises worthwhile. They contribute much to the quality of the pole ultimately carved, and both produce attractive results in themselves. These are carving an individual totem figure in low relief, for use as a wall plaque, to get the feel of the imagery possible, and whittling a small-scale model of a totem pole, to get a sense of work in the round and of how stacked forms relate to each other. Indians used this approach; masks and miniature poles are found wherever full-scale poles were carved.

To make a totem-mask wall plaque like the one shown above, you need a board of soft wood, such as a piece of ¾-inch pine about 1 by 2 feet; a craft knife; a pair of C-clamps; sandpaper; clear varnish, wood stain, or boiled linseed oil; and picture-hanging hardware—screw eyes, wire, and a nail. I have used this project many times with retarded schoolchildren, who often produce astonishingly vivid images. This project is based on a design by one such child.

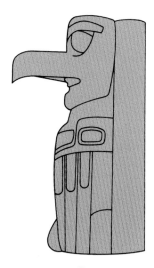

Raven

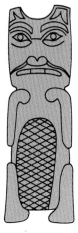

Beaver

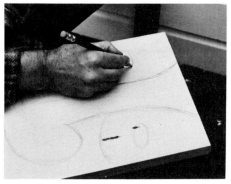

1: To begin a totem-mask wall plaque, sketch the face you wish to make on a piece of wood, using a pencil. Include all details, but keep the design simple. Before you start to carve, check the sketch for symmetry and balance.

2: Clamp the wood to a work surface and carve grooves about ½ inch deep along all the pencil lines. For safety and firm control, hold the craft knife with two hands, as shown, getting the free hand out of harm's way.

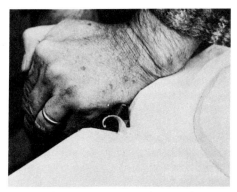

3: Using the craft knife, remove any wood that lies outside the edges of the pencil sketch. Pare it away gradually in thin chips, rather than trying to cut away large chunks.

4: If necessary, sand the finished mask. Then coat it with clear varnish, wood stain, or boiled linseed oil. You may want to try painting a mask with bright colors.

The Design

In a mask or totem image, horizontal symmetry and vertical balance are important design elements. Of course, you could incorporate all sorts of lopsided grimaces, but if these are unintentional they detract from the overall effect. For this reason, I always make a detailed pencil sketch of the mask first (photograph 1). (For design inspiration, you will find many ideas in the photographs and drawings shown on these pages.)

Make your pencil drawing right on the wood; only when you are satisfied with it should you begin to carve. I clamp the board to a railing on my back porch, but any comfortable work surface would do. To cut low-relief or small-scale carvings, I use a craft knife rather than a mallet and chisel, reserving the latter for full-scale totem poles. A craft knife gives better control. For maximum safety, grip the knife firmly in your right hand (assuming you are right-handed) with your right index finger extended along the top of the handle. Then cup your left hand over your right (photograph 2). This two-handed carving method not only gives good control, it gets the free hand—the one that usually suffers in an accident—out of harm's way.

The trick in carving a mask is to do no more knife work than necessary. Ninety percent of the board remains unworked. Your aim is to carve deep V-shaped grooves along the pencil outlines, then feather these grooves into the flat areas. With the knife blade inclined at a 30- to 45-degree angle, cut along the pencil lines. Lean first to one side of the line, then to the other, to cut the V-shaped channels (photograph 2). Then gradually whittle away any part of the board that lies outside the mask outline. Shave the wood away bit by bit (photograph 3). When the carving is completed, sand the wood and protect it with clear varnish, boiled linseed oil, or a wood stain (photograph 4). When the finish is dry, attach the fasteners and hang the mask on a wall.

Carving and Molding
A totem-pole miniature

¢ ⊠ ⅄ ⌘

A second project preliminary to making a full-sized totem pole is carving a scale model like the one pictured at right. This can be done simply for practice, as a test model for a big pole, or as a decorative object in its own right. The finished work can be attached to a broad base so it will stand by itself, be suspended from a ceiling, or be mounted on a wall. A doorframe is a good location.

A miniature totem pole gives you a chance to depart from traditional Indian figures in favor of a more personal style. In the carving at right, I sought a caricature effect. My self-portrait is at the top; my wife, a pet cat, and a Boy Scout are among the other cartoonlike figures.

A pole like this one is harder to make than a totem mask (page 2541) because you are carving in three dimensions. Use any long scrap of soft wood, perhaps 1-by-3-inch or 2-by-4-inch lumber. The length could be anywhere from 2 feet to 12 feet or more. The pole pictured is about 3 feet long. To begin, pencil a complete, detailed outline of the carving on all sides of the wood strip (photograph 5). (It is not essential that you carve all sides, of course; traditional totem poles were rarely carved entirely in the round.)

Carving
It is awkward to clamp wood of this shape while carving it; so I hold the wood in one hand, the knife in the other, and always cut away from the wood-holding hand. (I do not recommend this project for children, since it is sometimes hard to impress this point on them.) Such whittling is not as difficult as it looks. Remove small flakes and shavings of wood, at least until you get the feel of the knife and the wood. With an hour's practice, many people can get the effects they want. Some general advice may be useful: if you are working with a rectangular board, round all the corners early in the carving process except where you want squareness (as in the hat brim in photograph 6). To make a deep indentation, shave the wood away gradually, rather than trying to cut out chunks. As you work, retain a strong central core of wood to forestall breakage. With such delicate work, never force the knife blade; if slight pressure fails to complete a cut, withdraw the blade and make the cut in smaller stages. Keep the knife blade as sharp as possible. For the whittler, a dull blade is a nuisance as well as a hazard. A honing stone is a good investment, but replacement blades for a craft knife are inexpensive, and each blade can be used twice by inverting it in the holder when one side becomes dull. Always keep your free hand behind the movement of the blade. When you complete the carving, sand the wood lightly; then finish it with paint, stain, varnish, or boiled linseed oil.

5: To make a miniature totem pole, first draw a detailed pencil outline on the wood. If you plan to carve in the round, draw the sides and back of each element as well as the front.

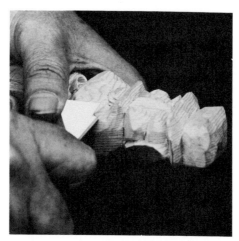

6: With shallow cuts, carve away deep areas such as the neck of this figure, leaving the raised areas such as the cheeks and chin. Then round off rough edges between, and the face will take shape.

This miniature totem pole, 3 feet long, was inspired by the work of Charlie Edensaw, a great Indian totem artist. Edensaw spent most of his life (1839-1924) making poles about this size:

The loon tree pole at Saxman Totem Park, Alaska, is a modern copy of a pole from Cape Fox Village, near Wrangell, Alaska. The loon flies overhead while three bear cubs scamper down to mother bear, who embraces her husband, a clan forefather. (The bear carving at the right has no relationship to the loon tree pole.)

The Sun and Raven pole, made in 1902, stands in Saxman Park, Alaska. The mythical hero, Raven, haloed by the sun, is at the top. According to the myth, he created light and the waters and visited the three children of the Sun (shown on his breast) during the Great Flood. In the center of the pole, Raven plummets earthward, with the sun's face at his tail. He dives toward Frog, who, according to the story, carried him to the bottom of the sea, where they saw many wonderful sights. To suggest this, three fish are shown on each side of the diving Raven.

The lower part of the Giant Rock Oyster pole at Saxman Totem Park, near Ketchikan, Alaska, memorializes a fisherman (right) who lost his life after a huge shellfish (left) clamped its jaws over his hand. His descendants took the Giant Rock Oyster as their clan totem.

The two photographs above picture the upper and lower halves of a totem pole at the Rochester Folk Art Guild in Middlesex, New York. Carved with hammers and chisels by guild members from a soft aspen tree, the images are composites of traditional totem motifs.

This totem pole was carved in 1965 by Cherokee Indians of North Carolina. It stands on the Shinnecock Indian Reservation near New York City. Such modern originals are made and sold by a number of Indian tribes unrelated to the original totem carvers.

Wolf

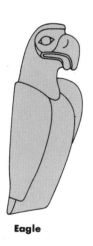

Eagle

This totem pole, 10 feet tall and 1 foot thick, was carved with only a mallet and chisel. If you make such a pole, you can model your images after the ones shown on these pages, but choose images that relate directly to you or your family.

Carving and Molding
A full-sized totem pole

A totem pole can take an infinite number of forms. The model for this project, shown above, is given only to suggest what is possible. In designing your pole, consider first the width and height you want it to be. Usually the dimensions are limited by the wood available. If a choice is possible, select the straightest pole you can find, preferably one with a diameter of 1 to 1½ feet.

7: Before you carve a full-scale totem pole, use chalk or crayon to draw the rough outlines of the individual figures on the peeled log. Don't attempt to draw in all the details at the start, for it is best to work the log first into a rough shape. Since the chisel will obliterate the chalk lines, details must be drawn in after the rough work is completed.

8: Using a mallet and chisel as pictured, with the cutting edge pointing away from you, make any deep indentations, such as those for the neck of a figure or between figures. If you are planning interaction between figures (as, for example, one standing on the shoulders of another), a dividing line is not needed.

9: Finally, proceed with the rounding and refining of each figure; here the top of a pole is being shaped. Carving rarely needs to go more than an inch deep. To make protruding parts, such as arms, cut out the wood adjacent to the area you wish to stand out. For large extensions, extra pieces of wood can be attached.

It is natural to want to erect the tallest pole possible, but where pole height is concerned, discretion is in order. Before you begin to carve, cut the pole to a length you can raise. Unless you have special equipment or many helping hands, a 10-foot length is about the practical limit for a pole 1 foot in diameter. (Even a log this size weighs several hundred pounds and must be raised with extreme care.) The way you erect the pole will determine how much of it you can cover with carving. If you plan to set the pole in a hole in the ground, the bottom quarter of its length should be left uncarved, for that much will be below ground level. This is the way the Indians erected poles, but it is an impermanent way, for ground moisture will rot the wood in time, and frost may cause the pole to tilt or even topple. To make it more secure, you can dig a hole 3 feet deep and 3 feet square; stand the pole in it, and pour concrete around the base. Put a bed of gravel under the pole for drainage.

Carving

Once you have decided how to raise the pole and have cut it to a length you can safely handle, choose the designs and sketch them on paper in the vertical sequence you like. Decide what height each figure will be, and check to be sure the total height equals the length of the area you intend to carve. Then select the face of the pole that has the fewest knots and other imperfections. With chalk or crayon, divide this face into measured sections that correspond to the dimensions you worked out in your drawing. Make a rough chalk sketch of the figure that is to occupy each section (photograph 7). Stand back and make sure you are satisfied with the overall appearance of the design—which may look different on the wood than it did on paper. Then, with mallet and chisel, begin the rough carving. First, make all the deep indentations that are necessary, such as the neck (photograph 8) of the topmost figure, pictured at left. Then proceed to the general shaping of heads and bodies. Photograph 9 shows the top of a pole being rounded. Once the crude outline is established, chalk in details such as facial parts, limbs, and so on, and chisel them away, little by little. Do not attempt to carve deeply. Totem poles are most effective in low relief. An inch or so is usually all that separates the deepest grooves from the uncarved surfaces.

Painting

When the carving is finished, coat the pole with a wood preservative and insect repellant such as creosote oil. Be especially generous with the preservative on the end grain, top and bottom, the most vulnerable to damage. When the preservative is dry, paint the pole in the brightest and most varied assortment of oil-based exterior paints that you can find. Two coats of paint, followed by a water-repellant clear varnish, will keep the pole bright for years.

For related projects and crafts see "American Indian Crafts," "Carving," "Heraldry," "Masks," "Sculpture," "Walking Sticks," "Wood Assemblages," and "Yard Environments."

TOYS
Wooden Entertainers

Steve Lindstedt, in addition to being a free-lance writer and song composer, is an incurable toy buff. A native Californian, he now lives in Garrison, New York, with his wife, Cecile, and his daughter, Skye, the latter an eager tester of any toy Steve makes.

Moonwinder

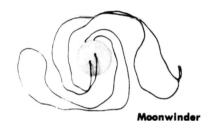

Wind the moonwinder by looping it around and around 30 or 40 times (top photograph), holding both ends of the looped string. Then start the button spinning by pulling the string taut (bottom photograph). By alternately relaxing and tightening the string, a youngster can keep the button spinning indefinitely.

Simple wooden toys seem perennially popular. Not only are they fad proof, but they have no metal parts to rust, no plastic to crack, no batteries to run down, no circuits to go awry. They are made of durable, workable wood that you can repair with a spot of glue or a paint touch-up. With the addition of string or rubber bands, small wooden toys can be made to perform in ways that delight children.

Equally delightful, from a parent's point of view, is the fact that traditional wooden toys can be made at home at little or no cost, and children can join in the fun of making them. Even the names are hard to resist. What child wouldn't want to show his friends a moonwinder, a bull roarer, or a gee-haw whimmy-diddle, particularly if it were a toy he had made himself?

The toys with these appealing names have long been popular in the Appalachian mountain regions of West Virginia, Tennessee, and Kentucky. In this area, famous for its handcrafting, store-bought toys are considered a luxury. For generations Appalachian parents have been making—and teaching their children to make—toys, using only simple hand tools, and following the procedures described here. For more advanced woodworkers are the non-Appalachian sports car, tug boat, and elephant trunk toys described on pages 2553 to 2558, and the hammer man on page 2559. These toys, too, can be handcrafted.

To make the toys shown here, you need: a coping saw; wood rasp; pocket knife; ruler; drill with bits to match the hole sizes specified; clamps; sandpaper in coarse, medium, and fine grades; all-purpose white glue; and a pencil. In addition, for the more elaborate toys, you need: a compass; square; hammer; and wire-cutting pliers. The wood, string or twine, finishes, and other special materials required are listed with each of the projects that follow.

Toys and Games
Moonwinder ¢ ▯ 👫 ✈

One of the oldest of the Appalachian toys (and one of the easiest to make) is the spinning wooden button called a moonwinder (shown at left). The button is threaded on a loop of string. To wind the toy, hold the ends of the string and loop the button around and around. To make the button start spinning, pull the string taut. After spinning the button in one direction, relax the string slightly so the button will rewind itself; then pull taut again. You can continue to wind and rewind it indefinitely by alternately tightening and relaxing the string loop.

To make a moonwinder, you need 4½ feet of mediumweight string or heavyweight mercerized-cotton crochet thread and a button cut from a dowel 1½ inches in diameter. (A round, smooth branch about the same diameter will do just as well.) Saw off a ¼-inch-thick slice of dowel (photograph 7, page 2553). Smooth its surfaces by rubbing it across sandpaper laid flat on the worktable. Match the 1½-inch mark on a ruler with the diameter of the button; then draw a diameter line across the button. Turn the button slightly and make a second diameter line. The point where the two diameter lines cross will be the center of the button. Mark hole locations ¼ inch on either side of the center and drill with a 1/16-inch bit.

Pass one end of the 4½-foot length of string through one drilled hole, then back through the other. Tie the two ends together with a double overhand knot. Spread the string loop between both hands, and let the button slide to the center of the string. Swing the button around in wide loops 30 or 40 times until the string is wound. To start the button spinning, pull your hands apart until the string is taut. Bring your hands in slightly to let the button rewind, pull apart to wind, in to rewind, and so on for as long as you want the button to spin.

This hardworking elephant may be ridden on, sat in, pushed, pulled, or used as a storage chest for other toys. With the lid off, as on page 2556, it makes a restful retreat for a weary youngster.

Bull roarer

Bull roarer

This bull roarer produces a low whirring noise as it is rapidly swung overhead in wide circles.

The bull roarer, also known as a howler, is a favorite among Appalachian children. When the shaped piece of wood at the end of a string is swung in circles overhead, as shown above, it makes a low whirring noise. Given the imagination of youngsters, that could account for the toy's name.

To make a bull roarer you need 25 inches of mediumweight cord, a 3/16-by-1½-by-6-inch piece of wood, and a 5-inch stick or length of dowel about ⅜ inch thick for a handle. Following Figure A, measure down ⅜ inch from the top along each edge of the wood slat and make a mark. Draw lines from the center of the top to these marks and saw along these lines. Drill a ⅛-inch hole 5/16 inch below the top point. Using a wood rasp, round and bevel the side edges of the wood (Figure A, side view). These edges are barely rounded near the top of the wood, but they become increasingly sharp until the bevels become a knife edge for the last 2 inches of the wood. Sand smooth, rounding the corners at top and bottom.

Pass the cord through the drilled hole and double knot the end. The handle at the other end of the cord is optional, but it makes the toy less tiring to use. In the ⅜-inch dowel or stick, drill a ⅛-inch hole ¾ inch from one end. Using a pocket knife or coping saw, cut a V-shaped notch in the same end. Slip the cord through the hole and double knot it over the notch. Fix the knots with a drop of glue.

To make the bull roar, hold the handle and swing the wood slat in circles above your head, making sure, of course, that no one else is within swinging range. Try different swinging speeds until you find the one that makes the wood vibrate so it gives the loudest roar.

A
Figure A: Front and side views show how the top of a bull roarer is shaped and drilled for a cord, and how the side edges are beveled to an increasingly sharp edge toward the bottom.

Gee-haw whimmy-diddle

There is a bit of mountain magic in the gee-haw whimmy-diddle, shown opposite (top right). You appear to make the propeller on the end of the stick spin to the right (gee) or to the left (haw) simply by telling it to gee or haw. (Gee and haw are the words Appalachian farmers use when they tell their horses or mules to turn to the right or the left.) The change in direction of the propeller is actually accomplished by a change in the position of thumb and index finger on the hand that rubs a stick across the notches of the propeller-bearing stick. But you can be the only one who knows this secret.

1: To notch a whimmy-diddle, mark the center of each notch with a vertical cut at ⅜-inch intervals; then make notches with diagonal cuts toward the bottom of each vertical cut.

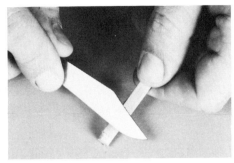

2: Remove wood from the center of the propeller, as shown in Figure B, by shaving it away from the dowel center toward the saw cuts near each end. Always cut away from yourself.

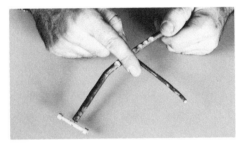

3: To make the propeller spin to the right, let the forefinger of your right hand touch the far side of the notched stick as you rub the small stick briskly back and forth across the notches.

4: To make the propeller spin to the left, put the forefinger of your right hand on top of the rubbing stick and let the right thumb touch the near side of the notched stick as you rub.

As one stick is rubbed briskly back and forth across the notches in the other stick, the propeller of the gee-haw whimmy-diddle starts spinning. When you know the secret, you can make it spin either right or left.

To make a gee-haw whimmy-diddle, you need: a 1⅝-inch length of ¼-inch dowel; a ½-inch common nail; and two branches, one ¼ by 8 inches and one ⅛ by 7 inches. Dowels may be substituted for the branches. If you use branches, square off both ends of each branch with a saw, and scrape off the bark and any knobby protrusions with a pocket knife, until you have a smooth, bare surface. (Always move the knife blade away from you rather than toward you.)

Measure 3 inches from one end of the 8-inch branch and make a pencil mark. Make additional marks at ⅜-inch intervals until you have seven in all. Place the branch flat on a table and use a pocket knife to make right-angled cuts, ⅛ inch deep, at each pencil mark. Then, starting ⅛ inch on either side of each of these cuts, make diagonal cuts down to the bottom of the first cuts to get the V-shaped notches shown in photograph 1.

With a pocket knife or coping saw, make four vertical cuts 1/16 inch deep and ⅛ inch in from each end of the 1⅝-inch dowel, two on each side (Figure B). Remove the wood between the cuts by carefully shaving from the center of the dowel toward each cut (photograph 2). You could also remove this wood with careful rasping, first on one side, then on the other. When you have achieved the elongated H shape shown in Figure B, drill a 1/16-inch hole through the center of the dowel from one flattened side to the other. Drill a matching hole, about 3/16 inch deep, into the center of the branch end closest to the notches. Using any hard surface, push the ½-inch nail through the hole in the propeller into the hole in the end of the notched branch. Don't push it in so tightly the propeller can't spin freely.

Geeing and Hawing

To make the propeller spin to the right when you command it to gee, take the smaller branch in your right hand and rub it rapidly back and forth across the notches in the large stick, held in the left hand, with the forefinger of your right hand positioned so it touches the far side of the notched branch (photograph 3). To make the propeller spin left when you command it to haw, place the forefinger of the right hand on top of the rubbing branch and let the right thumb touch the near side of the notches as you rub one stick briskly back and forth across the notches in the other stick (photograph 4).

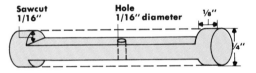

Sawcut 1/16″	Hole 1/16″ diameter	⅛″

B
Figure B: To make a whimmy-diddle propeller, first make shallow vertical saw cuts near each end on each side. Then remove the wood between the saw cuts with a knife or rasp until you have achieved this stretched-out H shape. Drill a nail hole in the center as indicated.

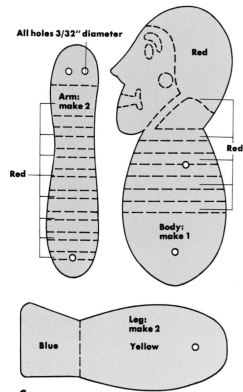

All holes 3/32" diameter

Red

Arm:
make 2

Red

Red

Body:
make 1

Leg:
make 2

Blue   Yellow

C
Figure C: When you copy these full-size patterns for the jumping jack parts, include the hole locations and the color guidelines. Trace the patterns on wood and cut them out with a coping saw. Note that you need two legs and two arms.

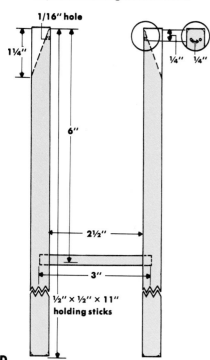

1/16" hole

1¼"

¼"   ¼"

6"

2½"

3"

½" × ½" × 11"
holding sticks

D
Figure D: Along the dashed lines, cut off the top corners of the sticks that will hold the jumping jack. Then drill parallel holes for the thread (end detail, right), and shallow holes for the dowel that will hold the two sticks together.

Toys and Games
Jumping jack

As the lower ends of the holding sticks are alternately squeezed and released, the jumping jack at the top end performs his backward and forward flips and his upside-down acrobatics.

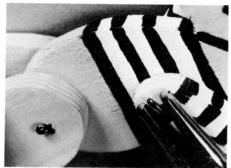

5: Attach the arms and legs to the body of the jumping jack by passing copper wire through the holes drilled in each part. Bend the ends over and pinch them against the wood.

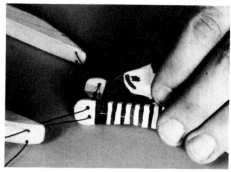

6: With the jumping jack laid flat, pass one end of thread through all the lower holes and the other end through all the upper holes. Then pull the thread taut and double knot the ends.

By squeezing the bottom of the holding sticks, as shown above, you can make this acrobat do handstands and around-the-world flips, forward and backward. To make this toy you need: one piece of wood 3/16 by 3 by 5 inches; one strip of wood ½ by ½ by 22⅛ inches; a ¼-inch dowel, 3 inches long; 2 inches of 15 gauge copper wire; and 8 inches of heavy thread.

Draw the acrobat pattern in Figure C (including the hole locations). Position and trace the five parts on the 3/16-by-3-by-5-inch piece of wood. Cut out these pieces with a coping saw, and drill the 3/32-inch holes. Sand each piece and paint it, following the colors pictured if you like. For extra decoration, I pasted a silver star on each boot.

Cut two 11-inch lengths from the ½-by-½-by-22⅛-inch strip of wood; these will be the holding sticks. With each stick lying on its side, draw slanted lines from its top inside tip to a point 1¼ inches down from its top outside tip (Figure D). Cut off these corners as marked. Drill parallel 1/16-inch holes as indicated through each slanted end, ¼ inch down from the tip and ¼ inch apart (Figure D, detail). Measure 6 inches down from the top of each stick, on the inside, and drill ¼-inch centered holes, only ¼ inch deep, for the dowel that will hold the two sticks together (Figure

D). Put a small amount of white glue in each hole, and insert the ¼-by-3-inch dowel. Clamp sticks and dowel together until the glue dries.

Place a leg on each side of the body, line up the drilled holes, and push a 1-inch length of copper wire through them. Bend the wire ends over and pinch them closed with a pliers. Repeat with the arms (photograph 5). Be sure the arms and legs can move freely. Lay the holding sticks down with the jumping jack on his back between the top ends (photograph 6). Pass one end of the thread through the lower holes in the left stick, left hand, right hand, and right stick. Pass the other end of the thread through all the upper holes. Tie the free ends of thread together with a double knot. Lift the assembly and alternately squeeze and release the bottom of the holding sticks. That will make the jumping jack do his acrobatics.

Toys and Games
Sports car

¢ ▣ ♦ ✈

The streamlined sports car pictured below (right) combines a modern appearance with an ageless simplicity. There are no sharp edges that might cut or scratch, and the toy is sturdy enough to withstand years of youthful batterings. To make it you need: one 1¾-by-2¼-by-7¼-inch piece of wood; a 5/16-inch dowel 5¾ inches long; and a 1⅜-inch dowel 2½ inches long. Enlarge the pattern (Figure E) and trace it, including the holes, on the block. Saw out the car. Drill the ⅝-inch hole for the car window and the two ⅜-inch holes for the axles. Cut four wheels, each ½ inch thick, from the 1⅜-inch dowel (photograph 7). Match the 1⅜-inch mark on a ruler with the diameter of each wheel and draw a diameter line. Turn each wheel slightly and draw a second diameter line. The two lines will cross at the center. Drill through each center with a 5/16-inch drill. From the 5/16-inch dowel, cut two sections 2⅞ inches long. Sand car, wheels, and axles with medium- and fine-grade sandpaper, making sure no sharp edges are left. Put glue on one end of each axle and tap on the wheel (photograph 8). Insert the axles through the car body and glue on the two remaining wheels. Finish with exterior-grade polyurethane or lacquer; make sure the finish is safe for use on toys that will be used by children.

Phil Greenblatt, his wife, Toby, and their son, Zach, live in a house that Phil built in Franklin, New York. Phil's love of woodworking led him to start his own business, the Handsome Brook Woodworks, which specializes in wooden toys. He also teaches woodworking at Hartwick College, Oneonta, New York.

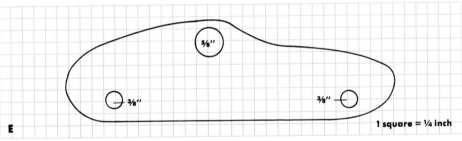

Figure E: To enlarge this sports car pattern, including the hole locations, draw a grid of ¼-inch squares; then copy the design onto the larger grid one square at a time.

7: To make sports car wheels or a moonwinder button (page 2548), cut off a disk of dowel with a coping saw.

8: With the sports car wheel flat on the work table, spread glue on the end of a dowel axle and tap it into the hole in the wheel.

Modern lines combined with simple, rugged construction make this sports car a popular and long-lasting plaything.

Stern-wheeler

When you wind up the rubber band powering the paddles on this stern-wheeler, it is ready for a cruise in the bathtub or on a pond.

A wooden paddle steamer, powered by a rubber band, makes a fine flagship for bathtub admirals. It can hold its own in a shallow outdoor pond, too, as pictured above. For the boat you need the following pieces of wood: ¾ by 5⅝ by 10⅛ inches for the hull; ¾ by 3⅝ by 4½ inches for the first deck; 1¾ by 2⅞ by 1 15/16 inches for the cabin block; ⅜ by 2¼ by 3¼ inches for the cabin roof; and 5/16 by 1⅞ by 3¼ inches for each part of the paddle. In addition, you need a stout rubber band and dowels of the following diameters and lengths: two ⅝ by 2½ inches; two ¼ by 1 7/16 inches; one ⅝ by 1¼ inches; and two ¼ by 1 inch.

Enlarge the patterns (Figure F) and trace each on the block of wood you obtained for it. Drill the ⅝-inch hole through the cabin block, and the ¼- and ⅜-inch holes in the hull and first deck. Put white glue in each hole; then insert the two dowel smokestacks, the single dowel in the front of the deck, and the two dowels that form the paddle mounts (photograph 9). Sand all pieces smooth and glue the first deck to the hull, centering it between the sides and locating the back edge 5/16 inch in front of the paddle-wheel cutout. Glue the cabin block to the first deck (photograph 10), centering it between the deck sides ⅜ inch in front of the smokestack dowels. Glue the cabin roof to the cabin block, centering it between the sides of the block and letting it overhang 3/16 inch in front.

Clamp the glued pieces together. While they are drying, saw the 5/16-inch slots in the two pieces that make up the paddle (Figure F). Slip one piece over the other (photograph 11) and tap them together (photograph 12). The fit should be snug but not so tight the pieces split; if necessary, sand the slots slightly before assembling.

When the glue has dried for two hours, drill two ¼-inch holes, each 1 inch deep, through the top of the cabin roof (Figure F). Put glue in these holes and tap in the ¼-by-1-inch dowels. The dowels will strengthen the joint between the cabin block and the cabin roof, important because children will pick up the boat by its roof. Give the boat a final sanding, rounding the corners and sloping the top of the roof slightly in front.

Place the rubber band around opposite inside corners of the paddle, hook it over the paddle-mount dowels (photograph 13), wind it up, and watch the stern-wheeler cruise. The boat may be left unfinished or given a coat of exterior polyurethane or lacquer. Make sure the finish is safe for use on children's playthings.

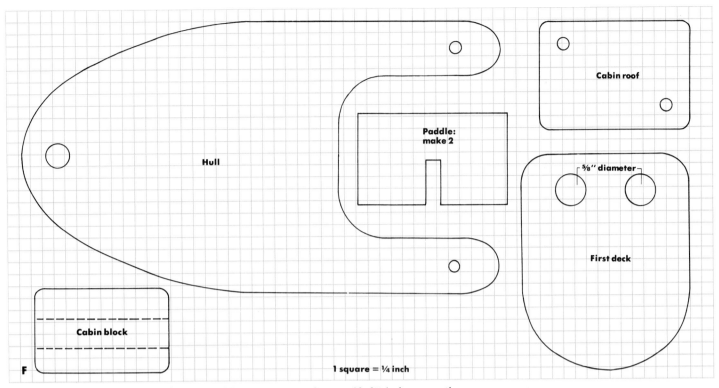

Hull

Paddle: make 2

Cabin roof

⅝" diameter

First deck

Cabin block

F

1 square = ¼ inch

Figure F: To enlarge these patterns for the paddle-steamer parts, draw a grid of ¼-inch squares; then copy the designs onto the grid, one square at a time. Transfer these enlarged patterns onto wood and saw out the pieces.

9: Dowels for the twin smokestacks, the front post, and the paddle-wheel mounts are glued into their respective holes before the deck and hull of the paddle steamer are assembled.

10: After you glue the deck to the hull, center the cabin block between the side edges of the deck, and ⅜ inch in front of the smokestacks. Then glue the block in place.

11: Cut matching slots in each part of the paddle wheel so you can slip them together until the center ends of the slots meet.

12: You can tap one paddle blade down over the other if the fit is snug. But don't force it too much; if necessary, sand the slots lightly.

13: With a rubber band in opposite corners of the paddle wheel, stretch the band until it slips onto the mounting posts on either side.

After riding atop an elephant, a youngster can rest awhile in the snug compartment inside. Note the removable lid that is resting against the side of the elephant.

Materials list, elephant toy chest

All wood can be pine except the wheels which should be a hard wood such as oak.

2 pieces ¾ by 11¼ by 23¾ inches (sides)

2 pieces ¾ by 5½ by 23¾ inches (sides)

2 pieces ¾ by 9¼ by 19⅝ inches (ends)

2 pieces ¾ by 9¼ by 14⅝ inches (body inserts)

2 pieces ¾ by ¾ by 22¼ inches (strips)

3 pieces ¾ by 1½ by 9¼ inches (lid inserts)

1 piece ¾ by 9¼ by 22¼ inches (floor)

1 piece ¾ by 5¼ by 8⅞ inches (ears)

12 pieces ¾ by 1⅝ by 4 inches (side slats at each end)

2 pieces ¾ by 2 by 4 inches (center slats at each end)*

6 pieces ¾ by 1⅝ by 15¾ inches (side slats on lid)

1 piece ¾ by 2 by 15¾ inches (center slats on lid)*

1 piece 1½ by 11½ by 20 inches (head)

1 hardwood piece ¾ by 4½ by 17 inches (wheels)

Two 48-inch lengths of ¼-inch-diameter dowel (pegs)

One 25-inch length of ⅝-inch-diameter dowel (axles)

½-inch-thick rope 1 foot long (tail)

*See page 2558 for how to cut center slats

Elephant toy chest

When the patient pachyderm shown at left and on page 2549 is not being pushed, ridden, or sat in, it doubles as a storage chest for toys. To make the elephant, you need the materials listed at left (below). Enlarge the patterns (Figure H) for the sides, ends, body inserts, and lid inserts; then trace them onto the pieces of wood cut for each. Cut each piece with a coping saw or saber saw. Since you need two of each (three in the case of the lid inserts), you can trace the first cutout piece on the additional pieces of wood to make sure the parts are identical.

When you have cut the four pieces that make the sides, edge-glue each upper piece (5½ inches wide) to a lower piece (11¼ inches wide) to make the two sides. Put glue on both joining edges and match each pair along the 23¾-inch length. If you have a pipe clamp or bar clamp or can rent or borrow one, use it to hold the two pieces together while the glue dries. If not, clamp them with a rope or buckled straps drawn tightly around the two pieces.

Drill the ¾-inch holes indicated for the axles, two in each body side. In the back piece of the elephant, drill a ⅝-inch hole for the rope that will form the elephant's tail. Slip an end of a 1-foot length of ½-inch rope through the hole and double knot it on the inside. Enlarge the pattern for the elephant's ear (Figure H), trace it on ¾-inch wood, and saw it out. Trace the cutout ear on a second piece of wood and saw that out. Enlarge and trace the pattern for the elephant's head (Figure H) on 1½-inch wood and saw it out.

Glue and clamp one ¾-by-¾-by-22¼-inch strip along each side, positioning it 3⅝ inches above the base or ⅛ inch above the cutout in the side. These strips will help support the ¾-by-9¼-by-22¼-inch floor. Now glue one side, one end, the floor, and its supporting strip together (photograph 14). Where the side overlaps the end, drill five ¼-inch dowel-peg holes, spaced as indicated in Figure G, through the side into the end piece.

Each of these holes—and all others you will drill for the pegs that fasten the elephant together—are drilled to a 1½-inch depth. As a guide, wrap a piece of masking tape around your ¼-inch drill bit 1⅝ inches from the tip; the extra ⅛ inch leaves space for the glue at the bottom of the hole.

Cut 36 pegs, 1½ inches long, of ¼-inch dowel. Put glue in each drilled hole and tap pegs into the holes. Clamp or apply a heavy weight to the joint while the glue dries. Join the side to the opposite end piece in the same way.

Locating Body Inserts

Before attaching the opposite side, draw lines across the floor 2½ inches in from each end, at right angles to the long edge of the floor. Draw corresponding lines (2½ inches in from either end) up the side that has already been fastened to the floor. On the side that has not been attached, draw lines 3¼ inches in from either end, at right angles to a long edge. These lines will locate the edge of the body insert nearest each end: you put these inserts in after both ends and both sides have been assembled.

Join the second side to the ends, floor, and supporting strip as you did the first, using glue and dowel pegs. This completes the basic box for the elephant's body. Slip the body inserts into the box, matching their front edges with the guidelines. Drill ¼-inch dowel-peg holes 1⅝ inches deep, spaced as indicated in Figure G, through the sides into the floor and the supporting strip. Put glue in each hole and tap 1½-inch pegs of ¼-inch dowel into the holes. Clamp or apply a heavy weight until the glue dries. Wipe off any excess glue.

Drill two ¼-inch holes in each of the twelve short ¾-by-⅝-by-4-inch slats that fit over the curved ends and body inserts at each end of the elephant, centering a hole ⅜ inch in from each end of each slat. Place the lowest slat so its holes are centered on one end piece and one body insert and its bottom edge is snug against the side of the elephant. Drill through the holes ¾ inch into the end and body insert, and glue and dowel the slat in place. Fit the next slat snug against the first, flush with the outside edges of the end and the body insert, and attach it as you did the first.

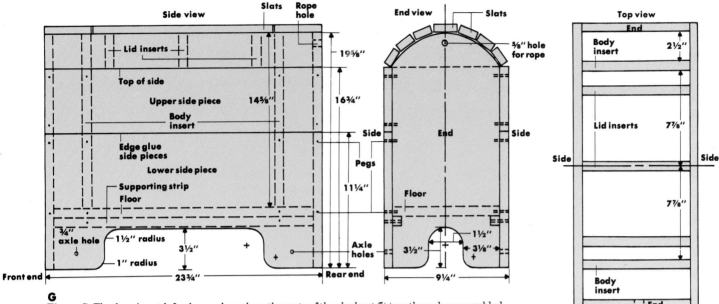

Figure G: The drawing at left, above, shows how the parts of the elephant fit together when assembled. The end view shows how the lid fits in the top of the elephant's body. At right is a top view showing the lid inserts. Patterns for all of these pieces are given in Figure H, below.

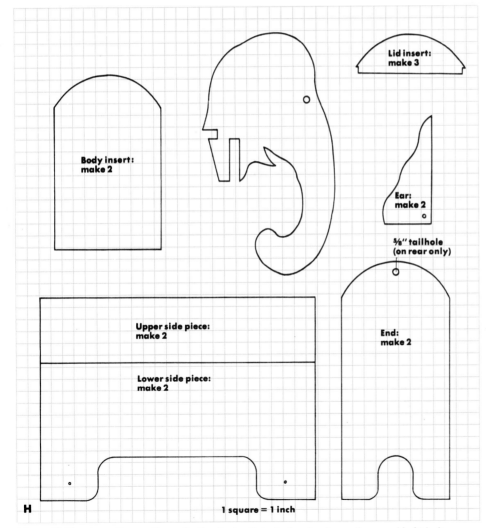

1 square = 1 inch

14: After gluing a supporting strip to the side of the elephant box, glue the side, an end, the floor, and the supporting strip together. Then reinforce the joint by connecting the side to the end with dowel pegs.

Figure H: To enlarge these patterns for the elephant's body, head and ears, draw a grid of 1-inch squares; then copy the designs onto the grid one square at a time. Transfer the enlarged designs onto wood and saw out the pieces. Use the first cutout ear as a pattern to trace the second ear.

15: After fitting six short slats to each end and body insert of the elephant, cut two slats to fit the opening that remains on each end. Attach the rear center slat, but not the front one until the elephant head is in place.

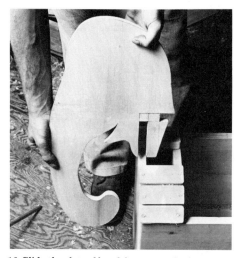

16: Slide the slotted head down over the front end piece; then notch the center slat cut to fit this opening so it will slide over the smaller side notch in the side of the elephant head, locking the head in place.

Attach the third slat. Then attach three slats on the opposite side and the six slats on the opposite end. In each case, work from the side of the elephant up toward the top of the curve.

There will be a space for a final center slat at the top of the curve on each end. Measure the width of this opening (it was 2 inches on my elephant); then cut slats to fit. Attach the rear slat with dowels and glue (as in photograph 15). Slip the elephant head into position at the front (photograph 16, left, below), centering it in the opening between slats. Cut a 1½-by-1⅞-inch slot in the slat you have prepared for the front opening. When the elephant head is fitted over the front end, the slotted center slat slides forward, locking the head in position. When you are satisfied with the fit of these pieces, glue the elephant head and the locking slat in position, putting glue on all adjacent surfaces. Fasten the rear end of the slat to the front body insert with glue and a dowel.

Glue the ears to the sides of the elephant head, locating them about ½ inch below the top of the head. Each ear should butt against the front of the elephant body. Drill the ¼-inch holes 1⅝ inches deep through the base of each ear (Figure H) into the front end piece. Put glue in the holes and insert dowel pegs.

Making the Wheels

Using a compass, press its point into the wood to mark the centers clearly and draw four 4-inch-diameter circles on the ¾-by-4½-by-17-inch piece of hardwood specified for the wheels. Cut out each circle with a coping saw and drill a ⅝-inch hole in the center. Cut two ⅝-by-12½-inch dowels and glue one end of each dowel into a wheel (keep the dowel end flush with the wheel's outer surface). Push the other end of the dowels through the ¾-inch holes drilled for wheels in the side of the elephant. Glue wheels to the free ends of the dowels.

17: Notches at the corners of the three lid inserts will rest on the elephant sides when the lid is in place. The two outside lid inserts are 1⅛ inches from the slat ends; each edge of the center insert is 7½ inches from an end.

18: The lid slats are glued and doweled to the three lid inserts. As you attach them, work from the sides up toward the center, and cut the final slat wide enough to fit the opening that remains at the top in the center of the lid.

Making the Lid

The lid for the elephant is made of seven ¾-by-15¾-inch slats, fitted around three lid inserts (photographs 17 and 18 and Figure G). Six of the seven slats are 1⅝ inches wide; the remaining slat is cut to fill the width remaining in the center, as were the center slats on the top of the elephant. On each of the six side slats, drill two ¼-inch holes in the center of the slat, 1⅜ inches from each end, and one ¼-inch hole, also centered on the slat, 7⅞ inches from one end.

Place the three inserts so their notched and flared corners rest on the elephant sides, with the two outside lid inserts 1⅛ inches from the body inserts on either end, and the edge of the center insert 7½ inches from the nearest edge of each body insert. Fit the lowest slat against the inserts, with its lower edge touching the side of the elephant. Make sure the holes in this slat line up with the center of each lid insert. When they do, drill through each hole into the lid insert to a depth of ⅞ inch. Put glue in the holes, and insert dowel pegs. Fit the second slat against the first and attach it the same way. Repeat with the third slat and the three slats on the opposite side. Measure the remaining space at the top of the lid, and cut a slat to this width to close the gap. Attach it as you did the others.

Give the entire elephant a final sanding and a coat of exterior-grade polyurethane or lacquer. Make sure the finish is safe for use on toys.

Toys and Games
Hammer man

Joe Borker started making wooden toys while he was attending the School of Visual Arts in Manhattan. He has a commercial wood shop which supplies stores in the New York area with wood sculptures, toys, and inlaid wooden clocks.

Materials list, hammer man
1 piece ¾ by 9¾ by 16¼ inches
(head and body)
1 piece ¾ by 3 by 12¼ inches
(arm and hand)
1 piece ¾ by 1½ by 12⅝ inches
(striking board)
1 piece ¾ by 3½ by 16 inches
(base)
1 piece 1 by 1 7/16 by 3¾ inches
(hammer head)
1 piece ½ by 1½ by 1½ inches
(cap for arm post)
1 piece ½ by 6¾ by 26½ inches
(wheels)
¼-inch dowel 7 inches long
(hammer handle)
¼-inch dowel 10 inches long
(axles)
⅜-inch dowel 2½ inches long
(arm post)
Wire coat hanger, two ½-inch common nails,
two 1½-inch-long No. 6 wood screws,
two 3-inch finishing nails,
primer paint and enamels
in colors indicated.

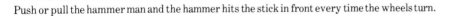

Push or pull the hammer man and the hammer hits the stick in front every time the wheels turn.

When this comical toy is pushed or pulled along the floor or sidewalk, it responds by striking the board in front with a hammer each time the wheels revolve. Although hammer man, as pictured above, is a colorful character, it is easy to build. To make it you need the materials listed at right (above). Enlarge the patterns in Figure I, page 2560, and transfer them onto the pieces of wood specified. Cut out the head and body, base, striking board, and the cap for the arm post, using a coping saw or saber saw on the curves. Before cutting out the arm, hand, and hammer head, drill the holes shown in the patterns of these pieces (Figure I). Also drill the hole for the arm socket in the body and in the cap for the arm post, and the ⅜-inch holes through the base for the axles. (If you don't have a long bit the right size, drill in from both sides of the base; if you measure carefully, the holes will meet in the middle.)

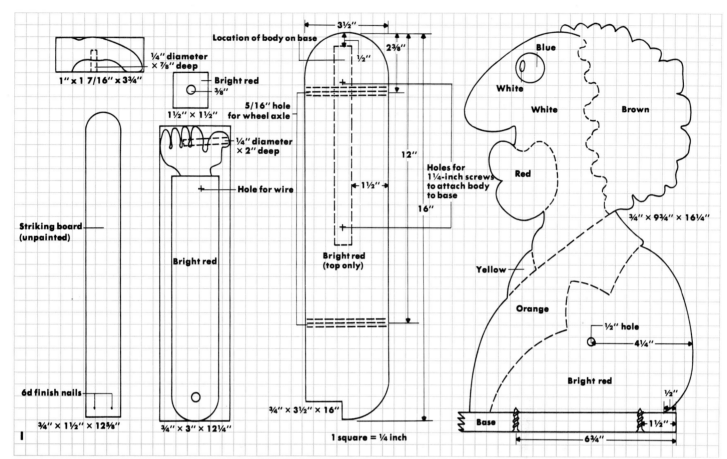

Figure I: To enlarge these patterns for the hammer man, draw a grid of ¼-inch squares; then copy the designs (including the hole locations and lines indicating the color patterns) onto the grid one square at a time. Transfer the enlarged designs onto wood and saw out the pieces.

Using a compass, scribe four circles 6½ inches in diameter on the ½-by-6¾-by-26½-inch piece, and use a coping saw or saber saw to cut out the wheels. Drill a ¼-inch hole through each wheel center. Sand all pieces and paint them as in Figure I.

Fit the striking board into the notch in the front of the base, and fasten it in place with glue and two 6-penny finishing nails. Position the head-and-body cutout on the base, following the guidelines indicated in Figure I; then glue and screw it in place with two 1½-inch No. 6 flathead screws. Drill pilot holes for the screws, and use a countersink bit so the screw heads can be driven flush with the wood. Glue a ⅜-inch dowel 2½ inches long in the hole in the arm; then pass it through the ½-inch hole in the body, and glue the arm-post cap on the other end.

From the 10-inch length of ¼-inch dowel, cut two 4⅝-inch lengths to make the axles. Glue one end of each axle into the center hole in a wheel. Pass an axle through each hole in the base and glue on the other wheels. Glue the hammer head to the 7-inch-long hammer handle dowel. Glue the other end of this dowel into the hand hole.

With a small nail or drill, make a 1/16-inch hole ½ inch in from the edge of the right front wheel. Make a similar hole in the hammer man's wrist. With wire-cutting pliers, cut a 10½-inch section from the straight part of a wire coat hanger. Use pliers or a vise to bend about ¾ inch of one tip of the wire at a right angle. Insert the bent tip in the hole in the front wheel, and use pliers to bend up the portion of the tip protruding through the inside of the hole so that the wire will stay in the hole but not so tightly that it will bind against the wood.

Where the wire clears the outside of the wheel, bend it toward the arm of the hammer man. When it reaches the arm, bend it back so it runs parallel with the front of the arm. With the hammer in its rear position and the wheel wire hole near the floor, let the wire extend ¼ inch past the hole in the wrist, but cut off any excess wire beyond that. Then bend the second tip at right angles so it will fit into the hole in the wrist. Staple the wire loosely to the wrist near the hole so the wire can move but will not slip out of the hole.

For related projects and entries, see "Preschool Projects," "Rockers and Cradles," and "Table Games."